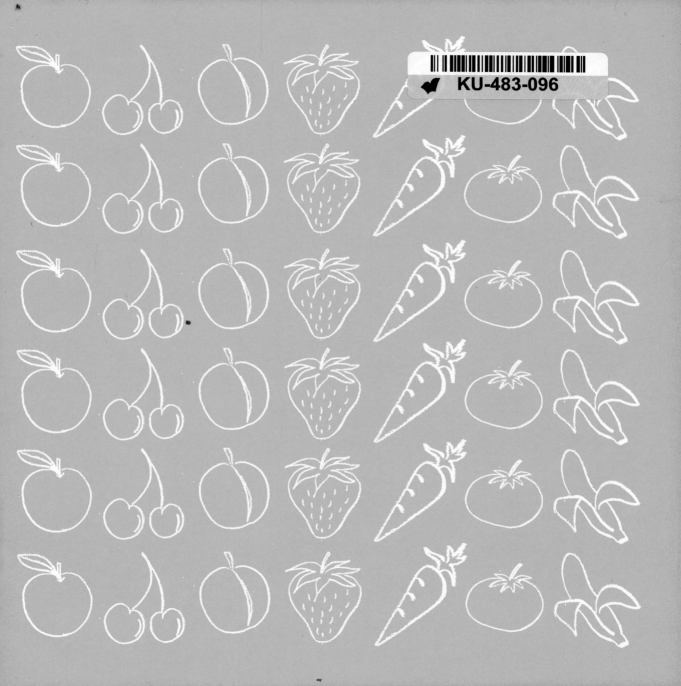

Sainsbury's Little ones

Recipes & nutrition

Essential recipes & advice from pregnancy to pre-school

ANNIE DENNY (PICTURED RIGHT)
Annie is a qualified Public Health Nutritionist at Sainsbury's. Annie has a passion for food and a wealth of experience in infant and maternal nutrition.

SARA STANNER (LEFT)
Sara is a registered Public Health Nutritionist and Science Programme Manager with the British Nutrition Foundation. She is also a mum of two.

Welcome!

Right from the start, what your child eats affects their health – not just now, but also in the years ahead. A good diet will provide all the nutrients and energy they need to grow and develop...

Feeding your children should be a fun experience for both you and them. That's where this book comes in with all the latest, up-to-date nutritional advice you need to give your little ones the best start in life.

Following your parenting journey from pregnancy through the early years of your children's lives, this book covers everything from what to eat when you're pregnant to the low-down on breast and bottle feeding, before moving onto a step-by-step guide to first foods, weaning and beyond.

It also contains a treasure trove of brilliant recipes to see you through the pregnancy and breastfeeding stages, plus easy purées and finger foods for successful weaning and a fantastic array of meals you can easily adapt so all the family can enjoy them. Best of all, you don't have to be a kitchen expert to make them as they all use readily available ingredients and have easy-to-follow instructions.

Each recipe has been tried, tested and tasted for guaranteed results. And you can be assured that all the nutritional advice and recipes have been checked by the British Nutrition Foundation and Sainsbury's nutritionists to ensure they meet the whole family's dietary needs. Happy reading!

Annie & Sara

Sainsbury's Little ones baby & toddler club
The Little ones website and baby club are great ways to get extra support at every stage of your baby's development. They offer expert advice, brilliant recipes and great offers. Join today at www.sainsburys.co.uk/littleones.

Contents

Before you get started...

This book is packed with loads of brilliant recipes and valuable nutrition information for both you and your growing family. Before you begin, here are some advice and tips to help you prepare and serve food safely and what to look out for in the book.

Hygiene and general safety

Following a few simple general rules will help keep you and your little ones safe and healthy when they're eating or around food in the kitchen.

✳ Always wash your hands well before preparing food and after touching raw meat.

✳ Teach children to wash their hands after touching pets and going to the toilet, and before as well as after eating.

✳ Keep surfaces clean and keep any pets away from food or surfaces where food is prepared.

✳ Keep chopping boards and utensils thoroughly clean.

✳ Keep cooked and raw meats covered and away from each other and from other foods in the fridge.

✳ Never leave your baby alone when they are eating or drinking. They should always be supervised.

✳ Thoroughly wash all bowls and spoons used for feeding in hot soapy water. Rinse well.

✳ Don't save and reuse foods that your child has half eaten.

✳ When cooking or reheating food, make sure it's piping hot all the way through, then let it cool down until lukewarm before giving it to your child.

✳ If using a microwave, always stir the food and check the temperature before feeding it to your child as there may be hot spots.

✳ Don't reheat cooked food more than once.

✳ Wash fruit and vegetables and peel as necessary.

✳ Pregnant and breastfeeding women and young children should avoid raw eggs, including uncooked cake mixture, home-made mayonnaise, ice creams and mousses or desserts that contain uncooked egg. Cook eggs until the yolk and the white are firm.

✳ Avoid giving your child honey for the first 12 months as, occasionally, it can contain bacteria that can produce toxins in a baby's intestines leading to a very serious illness (infant botulism).

✳ Don't give children food or drink when they're on the potty.

There's more age and stage specific advice in every chapter.

Storing, freezing and re-heating food

When you see this symbol with a recipe in this book, it means the dish is suitable for freezing. Unless otherwise stated on the recipe, here's what you should do to safely freeze or store food in the fridge, and reheat it.

1 Cool food as quickly as possible (ideally within one to two hours) and put it in the fridge or freezer. When freezing food, wrap it securely in clingfilm and kitchen foil, or place in freezerproof containers or freezer bags. Do not overfill containers. Squeeze out as much air as you can if wrapping or using bags. If possible, freeze in portions of the size you intend to use. Label packages with the date the food is frozen.

2 Food placed in the fridge should be eaten within two days. Frozen food should be thoroughly defrosted before reheating. The safest way to do this is to leave it in the fridge overnight or use the defrost setting on a microwave.

3 Reheat food thoroughly so it is piping hot all the way through, but remember to let it cool down before giving it to your baby. To cool food quickly, put it in an airtight container and hold it under a cold running tap. Stir it from time to time so that it cools consistently all the way through.

Vegetarian options

V Recipes with this icon are suitable for vegetarians.

For more information, advice and recipes, visit
www.sainsburys.co.uk/littleones

Kids can help

Recipes with this symbol are suitable for children to help make. Always supervise children and keep them away from ovens, hobs and dangerous utensils. See p163 for more about kitchen safety.

Nutritional information

We have only included a breakdown of nutritional values for the adult recipes. However, all the recipes have been checked by the British Nutrition Foundation (BNF) to ensure they are suitable for babies, toddlers and families. The BNF, along with Sainsbury's nutrition team, have checked all the nutritional text in the book to ensure it complies with the latest nutritional guidelines. All nutritional information is correct as of July 2011.

‘ *Discovering I was pregnant with twins came as a big surprise, especially as I already have a very active toddler at home* ’

Keely Hart, Mum to Daniel, 3, and pregnant with twins

You, pregnancy and food

Congratulations you're having a baby!

MY STORY

'I don't recall eating for two when I was pregnant but somehow I went from a svelte size 12 to Mr Blobby in nine months. By the time I was full term, I realised I'd put on 17kg! And it wasn't all baby as Lucas was just over 3kg when he was born. Luckily, I'm a keen sporty and a few (quite a few!) months later I'm now lighter than I was before I got pregnant.'

**Julie Schippers,
Mum to Lucas, 14 months**

You know that 'eating for two' is out-dated, but how much should you eat when you're pregnant? What foods do you need to avoid? Is there anything you should be eating more of? If you're feeling bombarded by healthy eating advice, don't panic. It can seem overwhelming at first, but a healthy pregnancy diet doesn't have to be complicated.

There's no doubt that healthy eating in pregnancy is important and can impact on how your baby develops. It's also vital for you, too, to stay healthy, both as a new mum and in the longer term. But you don't need to be perfect 100 per cent of the time – cravings, tiredness, nausea and changing tastebuds make that virtually impossible! Aim to eat a nutritious diet 80 per cent of the time, and you can't go far wrong.

If your diet is already well-balanced, it'll only take a few tweaks to make it ideal for you and your growing baby. But if you know your diet could be healthier, this is a great time to give it an upgrade. Here's your guide to the key foods to add – and avoid – in pregnancy, plus tips on how to adapt trimester-by-trimester.

First trimester
(up to week 13)
You shouldn't need to eat any more than normal. But many women feel hungry right from day one! Having three moderate meals and two to three healthy snacks a day will keep hunger at bay. Choosing wholegrain bread, rice, pasta and breakfast cereals can help you feel fuller for longer and, as a bonus, the extra fibre helps prevent constipation. Try snacking on unsweetened wholegrain breakfast cereals or wholemeal toast. During your first trimester, you may notice a metallic taste in your mouth and a heightened sense of smell that can put you off some foods – you may find eating sour or slightly acidic foods, such as pickles or citrus fruit, can help counter this. And contrary to common belief, cravings don't

SUPPLEMENTARY BENEFITS

A healthy balanced diet should provide you with all the nutrients you need, with two exceptions – folic acid and vitamin D. It's recommended you take at least 400 micrograms of folic acid a day, ideally from when you first start trying for a baby, and in the first 12 weeks of pregnancy. Folic acid reduces the risk of your baby developing a neural tube defect, such as spina bifida. You also need a 10-microgram supplement of vitamin D each day as it helps your baby make healthy bones. If morning sickness or cravings are affecting your eating habits, a multi-vitamin can help. If you don't eat any fish, consider an omega-3 supplement too. Choose pregnancy-specific products because general supplements contain vitamin A, too much of which may cause birth defects.

MY STORY

'It's hard to be good about what you eat when you're pregnant – especially when you love salt and vinegar crisps! But I have a pretty good diet overall so I think the odd treat is just fine.'

Mum-to-be Keely Hart

mean the food you want is essential for your baby.

Second trimester
(weeks 13 to 26)
It's only in the last trimester of your pregnancy that you might need to add an extra 200 calories a day to your diet. But if you're very active, or were underweight before you got pregnant, you may need to eat a little more at this stage too – ask your GP for advice. Food cravings and nausea should reduce, so you can enjoy food again. Weight gain tends to be more noticeable from week 20.

Third trimester
(week 26 onwards)
Your energy needs increase during the final three months, so you'll need to add an extra 200 calories a day if you haven't already. Tempting as it may be to add an extra sweet treat every day, try a nutrient-packed snack instead. Try two slices of wholemeal toast spread with peanut butter, a probiotic yogurt with a banana, a handful of dried fruit and unsalted nuts or oatcakes spread with houmous.

A growing baby means less room for food in your tummy, which can lead to heartburn. You might find eating little and often best at this stage.

Beat morning sickness
More than half of all mums-to-be will experience morning sickness during pregnancy. It's associated with changes in hormone levels, and often happens in the first trimester.
● Don't avoid food – eat little and often.
● Nibbling on starchy foods may help. Try oat cakes, crackers, unbuttered wholemeal toast, tea cakes, cereal bars or pittas. Try slicing and freezing bananas, then sucking on the slices.
● Ginger can help to alleviate nausea – make your own ginger tea by steeping grated fresh ginger in hot water. Peppermint tea may also help.
● Nausea is often triggered by strong smells. Keep a hanky with a few drops of essential oil on it handy – lemon oil works well.

Q Is it true I need to give up peanuts?

A The latest Government advice is based on research that there's no clear evidence that eating peanuts during pregnancy affects the chances of your baby developing a peanut allergy. So unless you are allergic to peanuts yourself, you can eat peanuts as part of a healthy balanced diet during pregnancy and while breastfeeding.

Q Should I give in to my cravings?

A Most women experience some cravings during their pregnancy, often for sweet, salty or spicy foods – sometimes all three at the same time. Experts are unsure why cravings occur – they may be linked to hormonal changes in taste or dietary imbalance. A little bit of what you fancy is okay, even if it is pickled onions and ice cream! Try to indulge in moderation or, even better, substitute healthier options – have frozen yogurt rather than ice cream, or a low-calorie hot chocolate instead of a chocolate bar. Some women get strong cravings for unusual substances, such as toothpaste or ice – even coal! Don't give in to them – consult your doctor instead.

MY STORY

'During my first trimester, I craved soft summer fruits – strawberries, peaches and so on. One day, I was struggling up to our front door with the shopping bags trying to get the key in the lock, all the while with my mind on the nectarines in one of the bags. The more I thought of them, the harder it became to concentrate on opening the door. In the end, I just had to dump everything, rip open the net and sink my teeth into one right there and then!'

Melanie Holmes, mum to Maia, 15 months

The babyweight debate

You're not alone in worrying whether you're putting on too little or too much weight while you're pregnant. Many women think they need to eat for two and this can lead to putting on too much weight during pregnancy, especially if you become less active during your last trimester.

In fact, if you're less active, your body uses the energy you're no longer burning to support the development of your baby. So you may need very little extra food!

There's no doubt that undereating in pregnancy puts your own and your baby's health at risk. You're more likely to have a low birth-weight baby if you don't eat enough, and be at higher risk of pre-eclampsia and anaemia if you're under-nourished. So it's important to eat a varied, healthy diet.

There is no particular ideal number in terms of weight gain as it depends on your weight prior to pregnancy. Most women who have a BMI within the normal range before pregnancy gain around 10-12.5kg (22-28lb), putting most of the weight on after week 20.

Excessive weight gain can increase your risk of having a complicated birth or going overdue. It may also trigger diabetes, high blood pressure and pre-eclampsia, and make daily life more uncomfortable for you, so it's important not to overeat during pregnancy.

If you were very overweight before you became pregnant (for example, a BMI of 30 plus), you will need to gain less weight while pregnant, but you should not diet to lose weight during pregnancy. Diet clubs can support you in how to eat healthily with minimal weight gain in pregnancy. But if you want to join a diet club during pregnancy, you'll need a letter of referral from your GP or midwife.

Staying active by walking, cycling, swimming or doing antenatal yoga can help you control your weight, and may actually make labour easier. Don't start a new exercise programme during pregnancy without advice from a health professional.

After giving birth, your body needs time to recover and you shouldn't try to lose weight too soon or too fast. Dieting is not recommended while you are establishing breastfeeding as your body needs time to get a good milk supply going and trying to lose weight might affect this process. Wait at least six weeks after the birth before starting to exercise again and take it easy to start with. If you had a C-section or birth complications, check with your GP before you start.

What should I eat?

Here's a guide to what to include, what to cut down on, and what to cut out when you're pregnant

 Good foods to include:

● **At least five portions of fruit** and veg a day. Frozen, dried and tinned counts too, and make useful standbys when you're short of time.

● **Dark green vegetables** such as spinach, watercress, kale or broccoli. A daily serving of these with your main meal will boost iron intake, plus they provide folate (the natural form of folic acid), which reduces the risk of spina bifida in babies. Wash well before use.

● **Fruit rich in vitamin C,** like berries, oranges, grapefruits and melon, to help support your immune system.

● **Wholegrain** varieties of bread, pasta or rice with every meal to provide fibre and B vitamins.

● **Good-quality protein,** such as chicken, fish, dairy products, eggs, nuts, seeds or pulses with every meal. If you're a vegetarian, eat a variety of protein-rich foods to get the full spectrum of amino acids (the building blocks of protein).

● **Dairy products** such as milk, hard cheese and yogurt, or calcium-fortified, non-dairy alternatives, to supply bone-building calcium and vitamin D for you and your baby. Lower fat options have fewer calories but as much calcium.

● **At least eight glasses of fluid,** including plenty of water. Good hydration will keep energy levels up and stave off constipation. Water, milk and unsweetened juices are good choices when you're pregnant.

● **Up to two portions of fish a week,** with one being oily fish such as salmon, mackerel, herrings and sardines. These are a good source of omega-3 fatty acids, important for the healthy development of your baby's brain and eyes. But limit tuna to no more than two small steaks or four medium tins a week. If you don't eat oily fish, consider a pregnancy-specific omega-3 supplement (that does not contain vitamin A) and include walnuts, linseeds and rapeseed oil in your diet. Note, you don't need to avoid eating smoked salmon unless you have a specific concern.

● **Lean cuts of red meat twice a week.** You need extra iron to prevent anaemia and to help you make additional blood. Iron in red meat is the easiest to absorb. If you're a vegetarian and at risk of anaemia your doctor may recommend an iron supplement.

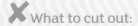 What to cut out:

Alcohol The Department of Health advises women not to drink alcohol, particularly in the first three months of pregnancy. If you choose to drink, have no more than two units a week after the first trimester.

Pâté and mould ripened soft cheeses, such as Brie, Camembert, soft blue and goats' cheeses as these may contain *Listeria*, a bacteria that can harm your baby's development.

Unpasteurised milk and foods made from unpasteurised milk, such as goats' cheese, can contain bacteria that may cause food poisoning. You can eat soft cheeses made from pasteurised milk, such as ricotta, mozzarella and cottage cheese.

Foods containing raw egg or lightly cooked egg, like home-made mayonnaise, chocolate mousse, soft boiled eggs and spaghetti carbonara sauce, as there's a risk of *Salmonella*.

Raw fish, shellfish, meat and poultry can contain bacteria that may cause food poisoning. Ensure meat and poultry are well cooked.

Liver and its pâtés are high in vitamin A. Too much of which can harm your baby's development.

Marlin, shark and swordfish have high levels of mercury, which can damage a baby's nervous system.

Foods to cut down on:

● **Caffeine** – high levels have been linked to miscarriage and low birth-weight. Stick to two mugs of tea or two cups of instant coffee a day. Some soft drinks are also caffeinated.

● **Snacks** that are high in sugar, salt or saturated fat. Choose ones that provide nutrients such as iron or folate, like unsweetened fortified breakfast cereals.

Haddock with crouton and herb crust

The herby crumb topping turns a plain fish fillet into something really special – and it's so quick and easy

Olive oil, for greasing and brushing
1 pack Sainsbury's haddock fillets
½ bag (about 45g) Sainsbury's sea salt and crushed black pepper croutons
Handful chopped fresh herbs, such as parsley or thyme leaves

1 Preheat the oven to 180°C, fan 160°C, gas 4. Lightly grease a baking sheet with some olive oil and put the haddock fillets, skin-side down, on the sheet. Lightly brush the top of the fish with olive oil.
2 Put the croutons into a strong plastic bag and bash with a rolling pin or crush with your hands.
3 Add the chopped fresh herbs and shake to mix together, then sprinkle over the fish – the oil will help the crumbs stick to the fish.
4 Bake in the oven for 10-15 mins until the fish is cooked through and the topping is slightly golden. Serve with steamed green beans and boiled new potatoes.

Per serving: 246 cals, 7.3g fat, 0.9g sat fat, 1g total sugars, 0.5g salt

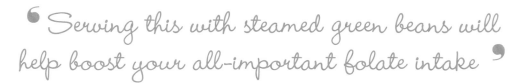

'Serving this with steamed green beans will help boost your all-important folate intake'

ANNIE DENNY, SAINSBURY'S NUTRITIONIST

SERVES 2
PREP TIME: 10 MINS
COOK TIME: 25 MINS

Chicken with mozzarella and spinach

Spinach provides folate – which is essential for first trimester mums and their growing babies. Chicken thighs are tender, flavoursome, offer great value for money and cook quickly

4 Sainsbury's Taste the Difference woodland British free-range skinless chicken thigh fillets
4 tsp Sainsbury's sundried tomato purée
2 handfuls fresh baby spinach leaves, washed
½ x 125g ball Sainsbury's SO organic mozzarella cheese or Sainsbury's Basics mozzarella cheese
1 tbsp olive oil
Salad, to serve

1 Preheat the oven to 180°C, fan 160°C, gas 4. Open out each chicken thigh fillet and spread 1 tsp of the sundried tomato purée over the inside of each one. Put a quarter of the spinach leaves on top of the purée, then tear the mozzarella into pieces and divide evenly between the chicken thighs, putting the pieces on top of the spinach.
2 Fold the chicken thighs over and secure with a wooden cocktail stick to hold the filling inside.
3 Heat the oil in a heavy-based ovenproof pan until hot, then put the chicken pieces in the pan with the join facing up and cook for about 5 mins without turning. Turn the chicken pieces over and put the pan into the oven for 15-20 mins or until the chicken is cooked through.
4 Serve with a salad of rocket, tomatoes and strips of cucumber.

Per serving: 460 cals, 26.1g fat, 9g sat fat, 0.7g total sugars, 0.6g salt

MAKES 4 BURGERS
PREP TIME: 15 MINS,
PLUS CHILLING
COOK TIME: 15 MINS

Home-made cheeseburgers

Fry or grill the burgers, then pile into a bun with as much salad as you like. Red meat such as beef has plenty of iron, which you need more of when you're pregnant to make healthy red blood cells

1 small onion, finely
chopped
2 tsp olive oil
500g pack Sainsbury's
Taste the Difference
traditional British
beef mince
30g Cheddar cheese, cut
into small cubes
1 free-range egg, beaten
4 Sainsbury's white
burger buns

1 In a frying pan, fry the onion gently in 1 tsp oil for about 5 mins or until really soft. Put into a bowl and leave to cool slightly.
2 Add the mince, cheese, egg and some freshly ground black pepper, and mix together.
3 Shape the mixture into 4 evenly sized burgers. Put them onto a plate, cover, and put into the fridge for 30 mins.
4 Heat the rest of the oil in the frying pan and fry the burgers, or grill under a hot grill, for 4-5 mins each side, or until cooked through and no pink colour remains. Put each one in a burger bun and serve with tomatoes, lettuce and relishes of your choice.

Per serving: 580 cals, 30.4g fat, 12.1g sat fat, 2.8g total sugars, 1.2g salt

Keely says: *'I have low iron levels at the moment so eating more red meat is good for me. Needless to say, my husband and son loved this meal – clean plates all round!'*

Baked leek, courgette and salmon risotto

This supper is packed with flavour and goodness. Salmon provides omega-3, which is important for the healthy development of babies' brains

15g butter

1 tbsp olive oil

1 leek, finely chopped

1 garlic clove, peeled and crushed

1 large courgette, trimmed and cut into 6mm cubes

175g Sainsbury's arborio risotto rice

600ml low-salt vegetable stock or water

1 pack Sainsbury's Basics salmon fillets, cut into chunks

25g Parmesan cheese, grated

1 Preheat the oven to 180°C, fan 160°C, gas 4. Heat the butter and oil in a pan and gently sauté the chopped leek for about 10 mins until soft. Add the garlic, courgette and rice, and stir so the rice is coated with the butter mixture.

2 Add the stock or water, stir well and transfer to an ovenproof dish. Bake in the oven for 20 mins.

3 Remove the dish from the oven, add the salmon to the risotto and sprinkle over the Parmesan. Stir well and return to the oven to cook for another 5-7 mins until the rice and salmon are cooked through. Serve garnished with watercress.

Per serving: 702 cals, 29g fat, 10.1g sat fat, 2.8g total sugars, 0.4g salt

Baked peaches

SERVES 4. PREP TIME: 5 MINS. COOK TIME: 10-15 MINS

Preheat the oven to 180°C, fan 160°C, gas 4. Halve 6 peaches and put into an ovenproof dish, adding a drop of Sainsbury's Taste the Difference Madagascan vanilla extract into each. Sprinkle over 4 tsp light soft brown sugar and bake for 10-15 mins. Serve with natural yogurt.
Per serving: 103 cals, 0.2g fat, 0g sat fat, 21.2 total sugars, trace salt

Baked peaches

Smoothies

Give yourself a vitamin C boost with these irresistible smoothies

MELON REFRESHER (back right)

Scoop the flesh from 3 small or 2 large, ripe melons such as galia, cantaloupe, and honeydew. Whizz in a blender with 200ml fresh apple juice. Makes about 1.5 litres

Per 150ml serving: 41 cals, 0.2g fat, 0g sat fat, 8.7g total sugars, 0.2g salt

JUNGLE SMOOTHIE (back left)

Whizz together 480g Sainsbury's frozen tropical fruit salad or 500g Sainsbury's frozen summer fruits mix with 300ml freshly squeezed orange juice and 2 x 125g pots Sainsbury's 1% Fat Fabulously Fruity Apricot, Pineapple, Mango & Peach yogurt. Makes about 1 litre.

Per 250ml serving: 146 cals, 1.3g fat, 0.3g sat fat, 27.5g total sugars, 0.1g salt

BERRY PURPLE (front)

Whizz together 75g ready-cooked fresh beetroot with 100g each fresh raspberries and strawberries, and 150ml fresh apple juice. Makes about 300ml.

Per 150ml serving: 52 cals, 0.1g fat, 0g sat fat, 10.2g total sugars, 0g salt

SERVES 4
PREP TIME: 20 MINS
COOK TIME: 3 HOURS
45 MINS

Slow-cooked lamb with lentils and herbs

A really satisfying, tasty dish that provides a good balance of healthy veggies, lamb for protein and iron and lentils for fibre, plus folate – what a winner!

2 tbsp olive oil

Sainsbury's British half leg of lamb (about 880g in weight)

1 red onion, finely chopped

2 celery sticks, finely chopped

2 carrots, finely chopped

4-5 garlic cloves, peeled but left whole

20g pack fresh rosemary

400g tin Sainsbury's Taste the Difference cherry tomatoes

800ml low-salt stock (vegetable or lamb) or water

2 bay leaves

150g Sainsbury's lentilles vertes

1 Preheat the oven to 150°C, fan 130°C, gas 2. Heat the oil in a heavy-based casserole and sear the lamb until brown all over. Remove the lamb from the casserole, add the onion, celery and carrots, and gently sauté for 10 mins.
2 Cut 2 of the garlic cloves into small pieces and remove half the rosemary leaves from half the stalks and chop. Make small incisions all over the lamb with a sharp knife and push the garlic and rosemary leaves into the cuts.
3 Put the lamb back into the casserole and add the tomatoes, the stock or water, bay leaves and remaining rosemary sprigs. Bring to a simmer, cover the casserole with foil and put the casserole lid on top. Cook in the oven for 2½ hours.
4 Remove from the oven, add the lentilles and cook for another 30 mins. The lamb should be falling off the bone.
5 Remove any woody rosemary stalks. Take the meat off the bone and serve with the lentils and vegetables.

Per serving: 415 cals, 23.3g fat, 8.3g sat fat, 9.4g total sugars, 0.3g salt

 Suitable for freezing (see p7 for information)

Tip...
Try making these dessert cakes with mixed fresh berries instead of apricots, and serve with a little cream.

Little chocolate and apricot cakes

Treat yourself to one of these tasty dessert cakes – tinned fruit is a great storecupboard staple, and counts towards your 5-a-day

125g unsalted butter, softened, plus extra for greasing
300g tin Sainsbury's breakfast apricots
125g light soft brown sugar
2 tbsp cocoa powder
2 free-range eggs
115g self-raising flour
½ tsp baking powder
1 capful Sainsbury's Taste the Difference Madagascan vanilla extract
Sainsbury's natural yogurt (optional), to serve

1 Preheat the oven to 180°C, fan 160°C, gas 4. Grease a 12-hole muffin tin with a little butter.
2 Drain the apricots and put the juice into a bowl with half of the apricots. Cut the rest of the apricots into small pieces and set aside.
3 Put the butter, sugar, cocoa powder, eggs, flour, baking powder and vanilla extract into a bowl and beat together until well blended – you can do this by hand or use an electric hand whisk. Add the chopped apricots and stir well, then divide the mixture between the muffin tin holes and bake for 15-17 mins.
4 Serve the chocolate cakes with the remaining apricot halves, a little juice spooned over or by the side and some natural yogurt, if you like.

Per serving: 173 cals, 9.8g fat, 6g sat fat, 11.4 total sugars, 0.2g salt

 Suitable for freezing (see p7 for information)

' After a few hiccups, we've finally found our groove when it comes to a feeding routine '

**Helen Kettle,
Mum to Seb, 7 weeks**

Breast and bottle feeding

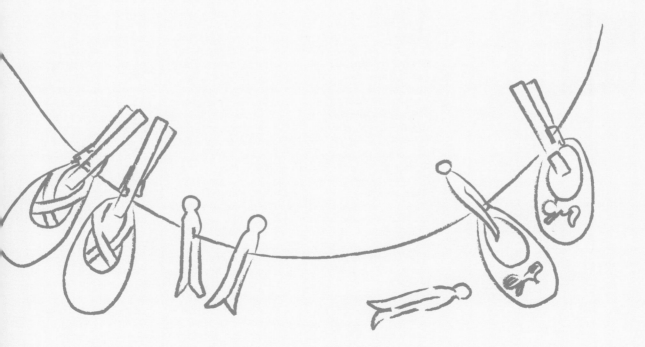

Feeding baby...
the milk stage

Breast milk is the perfect convenience food - it provides all your baby's nutritional needs on tap 24 hours a day, at the perfect temperature - and it never needs to be made up!

Why do the Department of Health and the World Health Organisation (WHO) recommend breast milk as your baby's sole source of food for the first six months? First, it helps develop a strong immune system, supporting your baby's ability to fight infection and disease. Exclusive breastfeeding may also help protect him from developing allergies and becoming obese when he's older.

The WHO recommends continuing to breastfeed for up to two years or beyond, alongside solid food from six months. Nature has thrown in bonuses for you, too. Producing breast milk uses up stored energy, which is why many women (but not all) find breastfeeding helps them to lose weight. Plus, it floods your brain with the hormone oxytocin, helping you feel calm and connected to your baby. Long-term, breastfeeding helps reduce your risk of breast and ovarian cancer.

Getting started

Lots of skin-to-skin contact as soon as possible after birth will encourage your baby to breastfeed. Many babies instinctively start to 'root' for the breast as soon as they are born. If your baby doesn't, encourage him to feed by holding him close, so his nose is level with your nipple. Then, if you gently lift his head and tilt it a little so the top lip brushes against your nipple, he should open his mouth. Bring him closer so he can fill his mouth with the breast, rather than just the nipple.

You'll feed better if you feel comfortable and your baby is calm. Feeding can take a long time, so gather everything you need around your favourite place to sit before you start. Mastering breastfeeding is a steep learning curve for both you and your baby, so relax, put your feet up and give your baby time to feed.

How much should I breastfeed?

You may feel like you have little milk at first, but allowing your baby to suckle as much as he wants will increase your milk production to match his needs. It's impossible to overfeed a baby with breastmilk, so be led by your baby and allow him to come off the breast when he's ready, then offer him the second breast. If you let your baby breastfeed on demand, he will get all the liquid he needs (though in very hot weather you may want to give cooled boiled water as an additional drink).

Looking after you

The best support you can give yourself when you're breastfeeding is to eat a good diet, with three meals a day and healthy snacks in between, and to keep well hydrated. Simple meals can be very nutritious – try a baked potato with baked beans or stir-fried chicken with vegetables. We've included quick and nutritious recipes in this chapter to inspire you. It is important to maintain an adequate intake of calcium and vitamin D while breastfeeding, both for your future bone health and your baby's development. If you eat fewer than five servings of dairy products (or calcium-enriched alternatives, such as calcium- enriched soya milk), you should consider a calcium supplement. We get most of our vitamin D from the effect

of sunlight on our skin, but it's also found in oily fish such as mackerel, sardines and salmon, as well as eggs and beef liver. Omega-3 fatty acids play an important role in the development of baby's brain and vision and these are also found in oily fish. You should aim to eat two servings of fish each week, one of which should be oily (but don't eat more than two portions of oily fish per week). If you can't, you may wish to take omega-3 and vitamin D supplements.

It is also important to keep well hydrated – drink an additional four to six glasses of fluid each day on top of your usual six to eight glasses. Alcohol and caffeine can pass into your milk, so you should avoid or limit your intake.

The body is very efficient at making breast milk but you may find your appetite increases. If it does, try to add nutritious snacks, such as low-fat yogurt or unsalted nuts and dried fruit. This is not the time to diet – if you skip meals or don't get enough nutrients, you'll quickly feel exhausted and it may affect your milk supply. Work towards a gradual weight-loss by steering clear of high-calorie indulgences,

maintaining a balanced diet and getting out for a brisk 30-minute walk every day as soon as you feel up to it.

What about allergies?

There is no need to avoid potentially allergenic foods during pregnancy or breastfeeding (unless you are allergic to the food yourself). If you do suspect that your baby is reacting to some foods you are consuming, and shows signs of food allergies or intolerances, discuss this with your GP. For more information on allergies, turn to p49.

Bottle feeding

If breastfeeding doesn't work for you and your baby, or if you choose not to breastfeed, don't give yourself a hard time. If you're not breastfeeding,

MY STORY

'Breastfeeding your baby is an amazing time. While I was breastfeeding my little boy I used to catch up on TV. It is a great time to have some closeness with your little one but also a great opportunity to have a bit of me-time!'

Yvette Newbatt, Mum to Oliver, 2½

MY STORY

'I breastfed Seb for the first two weeks but he had a tongue tie which made it difficult for him to latch on. By the time we got it sorted, he was so used to the bottle that we just stuck with it. Although breastfeeding was a lovely way to bond, Seb is happy with the bottle and it means Daddy can feed him too!' **Helen Kettle, Mum to Seb, 7 weeks**

Q Should I avoid any foods while breastfeeding?

A The foods you avoided during pregnancy, such as soft cheese, shellfish and pâté, are now fine to eat. Spicy foods are generally okay for most. The best advice is to carry on eating a varied and balanced diet. Either avoid alcohol or limit your intake, and don't consume too much caffeine – remember, it's found in some soft drinks and cold remedies, as well as tea and coffee. As far as peanuts are concerned, you don't need to avoid these, as recent research suggests that eating peanuts while breastfeeding has no effect on baby's chance of developing an allergy.

the only milk you should give your baby is infant formula specifically for babies under six months (not follow-on/stage 2 milk). Infant formulas are manufactured in line with strict legal composition guidelines to provide all the nutrients your baby needs.

Most formulas are based on ingredients made from cow's milk, and many include essential fats and prebiotics to mimic breast milk. Other 'normal' milks, such as cow's, goat's or sheep's milk, are not suitable for babies. Soya-based infant formulas should only be given on your doctor's advice.

Formula should be made up when you need it and according to the guidelines on the packaging. Always measure it accurately as too much powder can give your baby constipation and lead to dehydration, while too little can prevent him from getting the nutrients he needs.

You will need the right equipment, including a supply of bottles and the right teat for newborns. You'll also need brushes for bottle cleaning,

plus a sterilising unit, which can either be plugged in or used in the microwave.

If you're out, take a vacuum flask of just boiled water with you and a measured amount of formula in a container. You can also opt for ready-made cartons. Opened cartons can be kept in the fridge for up to 24 hours. Any unfinished bottles should be thrown away if they're not finished within an hour. Avoid warming formula in a microwave as this can produce hotspots that may burn baby's mouth.

Some women find mixed feeding – combining breast and bottle – works well, although it's usually best to wait until breastfeeding is established (after six to eight weeks) before introducing a bottle. Formula takes longer to digest than breast milk, and some mums find making the last feed at night a bottle feed helps their baby to sleep through. Stick to a regular feeding schedule and your breast milk production will adjust accordingly. But do note that your baby may stop

breastfeeding altogether if you introduce a bottle.

If you're bottlefeeding and think your baby may have a cow's milk allergy (symptoms include a rash, diarrhoea and failure to thrive), see your doctor or health visitor as soon as possible. Specialised baby formulas for infants with cow's milk allergy can be prescribed by a doctor.

Boiled, cooled tap water can be given to formula-fed babies from around six weeks. If sterilised tap water is not available, some bottled water is okay to use as long as it contains no more than 200mg of sodium per litre. Check the bottle label for info.

Other drinks can be given as your baby gets a bit older – try to start using a feeder beaker at around six months so baby doesn't become dependent on the bottle. Unsweetened fruit juices should be diluted one-part juice to 10 parts water and can be given to babies from six months. As with all drinks containing sugar, they are best kept to mealtimes.

Breastfeeding troubleshooting

Sometimes, breastfeeding doesn't go quite as smoothly as you might hope. But there's no reason to be anxious – there's plenty of advice and support to help you

Breastfeeding is 100 per cent natural but that doesn't mean it's always 100 per cent easy! Don't struggle in silence – there's a lot of support available, including drop-in breastfeeding clinics, and one-on-one advice from fully trained NHS lactation consultants or breastfeeding counsellors – speak to your midwife or health visitor to find your nearest. In the meantime, here's how to get over the most common feeding hurdles.

'Feeding is so painful'
Breasts are super-sensitive and many women are surprised at how powerfully a baby can suck, so the initial pain when a baby latches on can be a shock. But pain that persists throughout a feed is almost always due to incorrect positioning and can lead to cracked and sore nipples. If your nipples are very sore, expressing for 48 hours can give them a break, but the best thing you can do is get some advice about positioning. See below for where to get help. Sometimes, pain can be caused by thrush. See your GP to ask about anti-fungal treatment for you and your baby if he becomes fussy about feeding and his mouth is sore.

'I've got mastitis'
Sore nipples can lead to mastitis - if the breast is not fully emptied, milk can back up, causing lumpy sore spots on the breast. If untreated, it can lead to an infection and produce flu-like symptoms. See your GP as you may need antibiotics. Taking ibuprofen and resting may help to relieve symptoms, too.

'Feeding takes hours'
Be prepared for feeding to take a while in the first few weeks. But if you feel it's taking a very long time, get advice from a breastfeeding expert.

A baby may comfort himself sometimes with sucking rather than feeding - a breastfeeding expert will help you manage this. If you're feeling isolated, joining a local post-natal group can be a huge support.

It can be hard to juggle breastfeeding with looking after a toddler or other children, but involve them by sitting down together and reading a book while you feed. Cut yourself some slack and delegate as many household tasks to others as you can.

'I have leaky breasts after feeding'
Some women experience leaking and others don't. It's not a sign that anything is wrong – it's just a way for your body to relieve engorged breasts. Use breastpads to soak up any leaks and relieve engorged breasts with cooling pads.

'I'm not sure if I'm making enough milk'
Worrying about whether your baby is getting enough milk is often about confidence. The key thing is not to worry. If your baby is gaining weight and producing lots of wet nappies, then you're producing enough milk. Talk to your health visitor if you are concerned.
● **Expert advice from NHS Lactation Consultant Jane Gerard-Pearse**

Breastfeeding help
● *The National Breastfeeding Helpline is funded by the NHS and can help you find a local drop-in clinic, lactation consultant or breastfeeding counsellor. Call 0300 100 0212.*
● *The National Childbirth Trust (NCT) Breastfeeding Line is staffed by breastfeeding counsellors. Visit www.nct.org.uk to find your local branch. To contact a breastfeeding counsellor, call 0300 330 0771.*
● *The Breastfeeding Network (BfN) is an independent source of support and advice on all aspects of breastfeeding. Visit www.breastfeedingnetwork.org.uk.*

SERVES 2
PREP TIME: 5 MINS
COOK TIME: 15 MINS

Thai red curry noodle with stir-fried veg Ⓥ

This simple meat-free dish is loaded with fresh veg for extra vitamins and uses just one pan to make washing-up quick and easy

1 tbsp olive oil
1 medium red chilli, deseeded and finely sliced
1 tbsp Sainsbury's Thai red curry paste
150ml hot Sainsbury's Signature vegetable stock
410g pack Sainsbury's free-range fresh egg noodles
½ small onion, sliced
300g pack Sainsbury's crunchy vegetable stir fry
1 tbsp desiccated coconut, toasted in a dry frying pan for 1-2 mins

1 Heat half the olive oil in a wok over a high heat and add the chilli. Fry for a couple of mins and add the curry paste. Pour in the hot vegetable stock and bring to a simmer.
2 Add the noodles and heat for 3-4 mins. Remove and keep warm.
3 Heat the remaining oil in the wok over a high heat. Stir-fry the onion until it begins to colour then tip in the crunchy vegetable mix in and stir-fry for 2-3 mins until just wilted, adding a splash of water if necessary to help create steam.
4 To serve, arrange the noodles on each plate and top with the stir-fried vegetables. Garnish with a sprinkling of toasted coconut.
Per serving: 488 cals, 15.7g fat, 5.2g sat fat, 8.6g total sugars, 0.5g salt

Pancetta, mushroom and rocket pizza

The pizza base provides plenty of carbs for energy, while rocket provides calcium and folate, which are great for breastfeeding mums

145g Sainsbury's pizza base mix

Small knob unsalted butter

2 tsp olive oil

50g Sainsbury's cubetti di pancetta

10 Sainsbury's SO organic chestnut mushrooms or Sainsbury's closed cup chestnut mushrooms, finely sliced

2 tbsp tomato purée

2 tbsp Parmesan cheese, grated

2 handfuls fresh rocket

1 Preheat the oven to 220°C, fan 200°C, gas 7. Make up the pizza dough according to the pack instructions. Roll the dough out to a circle 25cm in diameter and transfer to a lightly greased baking tray.

2 Meanwhile, heat the butter and oil in a frying pan and cook the pancetta until just golden. Add the sliced mushrooms to the pan and cook for about 10 mins or until the mushrooms are golden.

3 Spread the tomato purée over the dough, then top with the mushroom mixture. Sprinkle over the Parmesan and bake for 15 mins or until cooked.

4 Scatter the rocket over the pizza and serve.

Per serving: 441 cals, 20g fat, 8.5g sat fat, 3.1g total sugars, 1.7g salt

French omelette with fine herbs

SERVES 1. PREP TIME: 10 MINS. COOK TIME: ABOUT 5 MINS

Melt ½ tbsp butter in a frying pan over a medium heat. Beat 3 eggs, 1 tbsp whole milk and 1 tsp each chopped fresh parsley and chives. Pour into the pan and cook for 3-4 mins or until the egg is fully cooked, pushing the edges into the centre as it starts to set. Fold and serve.
Per serving: 319 cals, 25g fat, 9.2g sat fat, 0.9g total sugars, 0.7g salt

French omelette with fine herbs

Hearty Waldorf salad

When you're feeding baby you don't have a lot of time to spend on feeding yourself. The solution? A supper that's ready in a flash and packed with lots of healthy, crunchy fruit and veg. Yum!

2 tbsp Sainsbury's
light mayonnaise
2 tbsp soured cream
Juice of ½ lemon
½ tsp caster sugar
1 red apple
100g red grapes, halved
½ celery stick, trimmed
and sliced
210g pack Sainsbury's Be
good to yourself cooked
roast chicken slices
½ head romaine lettuce
2 tbsp Sainsbury's
walnut pieces
Few sprigs Sainsbury's
fresh flat-leaf parsley,
chopped

1 In a large bowl, whisk together the mayonnaise, soured cream, lemon juice and sugar.
2 Core the apple and slice into thin wedges. Add to the dressing, along with the grapes and celery, then toss to coat.
3 Tear the chicken into bite-size pieces, then add to the bowl. Mix together until combined. Season.
4 Roughly tear the lettuce and arrange on plates. Top with the chicken mixture, a sprinkling of walnut pieces, chopped fresh parsley and freshly ground black pepper.

Per serving: 414 cals, 21.6g fat, 3.2g sat fat, 17.2g total sugars, 0.7g salt

Tip...
For a quick and easy midweek lunch for two, load any leftover Waldorf salad into wholemeal pitta breads.

SERVES 4
PREP TIME: 15 MINS
COOK TIME: 25 MINS

Chicken balti

A tasty curry with plenty of brightly coloured peppers and tomatoes. They both provide vitamin C, which is important for the immune system

1½ tbsp vegetable
or olive oil

1 onion, sliced

1 red and 1 orange pepper,
deseeded and diced

1 aubergine, trimmed and
cut into small chunks

4 Sainsbury's Taste the
Difference chicken thigh
fillets, cut into chunks

70g balti paste

400ml reduced fat
coconut milk

200g Sainsbury's chopped
tinned tomatoes

Handful fresh coriander
(optional)

1 Heat the oil in a pan over a low heat and fry the onion, peppers and aubergine for about 10 mins or until the onion is soft.

2 Add the chicken to the pan and stir-fry for a few more mins, then add the balti paste and cook for another few mins.

3 Add the coconut milk and tomatoes and simmer gently for 10 mins until the sauce has reduced slightly and the chicken is cooked through. Add a handful of fresh coriander (if using) and serve with rice or couscous, and naan bread.

Per serving: 324 cals, 21.7g fat, 12.1g sat fat, 10.9g total sugars, 0.8g salt

 Suitable for freezing (see p7 for information)

If you have concerns about the spice in the balti, simply use less paste in the recipe!

ANNIE DENNY, SAINSBURY'S NUTRITIONIST

Baked sea bass parcels with a fresh salsa

Time-pressed feeding mums need meals that are ready in minutes and packed with flavour. This delightfully easy supper is just the ticket!

Oil, for greasing
1 pack Sainsbury's boneless sea bass fillets (about 210g), or boneless cod fillets
Juice of ½ lemon
A little butter

FOR THE SALSA
1 tbsp Thai fish sauce
1 tbsp golden caster sugar
2 tbsp white wine vinegar
1 small ripe avocado
6 Sainsbury's Taste the Difference Vittoria cherry tomatoes
¼ cucumber
Juice of ½ lemon
Large handful chopped fresh coriander

1 Cut two pieces of kitchen foil, each big enough to wrap loosely around a fish fillet to make a parcel. Rub a little oil over the foil and put a sea bass fillet onto each piece. Squeeze the lemon juice over the fish, dot with butter and season with freshly ground black pepper.
2 Fold the foil over, seal the edges and bake for 12 mins. Open the parcel to check if the fish is cooked – it may need another 2-3 mins.
3 While the fish is cooking, make the salsa. Put the Thai fish sauce, sugar and vinegar into a small pan and heat gently until the sugar has dissolved. Turn up the heat and leave to bubble for a few mins until it has thickened slightly. Leave to cool.
4 Peel the avocado and remove its stone, then finely chop and put into a bowl. Finely chop the tomatoes and cucumber and add to the avocado with the lemon juice and coriander. Pour over the fish sauce mixture and mix gently.
5 Remove the fish from the parcels and serve with the salsa. You can also serve with mini jacket potatoes or crushed boiled potatoes, if you like.

Per serving: 317 cals, 19.8g fat, 6.9g sat fat, 10.2g total sugars, 1.8g salt

Easy raspberry cheesecake

Entertaining guests who've come to see the new arrival can be exhausting but this beautiful, show-stopping soft-set cheesecake is as easy to make as it is delicious to eat!

12 gingernut biscuits

50g unsalted butter, melted, plus a little extra for greasing

125g pot Sainsbury's 1% fat fabulously fruity heritage raspberry yogurt (from summer fruits pack of 4 yogurts)

200g light soft cream cheese

150ml pot double cream

150g pack Sainsbury's fresh raspberries

Icing sugar, to decorate

1 Put the gingernut biscuits into a strong bag and bash with a rolling pin or whizz in a food processor to make fine crumbs. Tip the crumbs into a bowl, add the melted butter and mix together.

2 Grease and line a 20cm diameter flan tin (one with a loose bottom is best) with greaseproof paper, tip in the crumb mixture and press down to form a firm, even base. Put into the fridge.

3 Meanwhile, mix together the yogurt and cream cheese in a large bowl. In another bowl, whip the cream to stiff peaks with an electric hand whisk.

4 Add the cream to the yogurt mixture along with most of the raspberries. Stir together, then spoon on to the biscuit base and smooth the top.

5 Leave to set in the fridge for at least 2 hours, preferably longer. Decorate with the remaining raspberries and sprinkle over icing sugar to serve.

Per serving: 460 cals, 39.7g fat, 24.6g sat fat, 12.1g total sugars, 0.4g salt

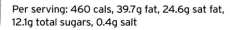

Helen says: *'This is really easy and delicious, and the gingernut biscuits really made it. I made mine in individual glasses and added a dessertspoon of sugar for a little extra sweetness!'*

'I had no idea motherhood would be so much fun! It's brilliant watching him learn how to be a little person'

Maria Onyango,
Mum to Theodore, 5½ months

Starting to wean

First foods

By six months, your baby should be ready to try solid food. Some babies seem ready for weaning between four and six months - if this is the case, try increasing her milk feeds first. Every baby is different - if you're thinking of introducing solids before six months, speak to your health visitor for advice. No solids should be given before four months (17 weeks), as a baby's digestive system is not fully developed by that stage.

Moving on from breastfeeding

Experts agree that keeping up breastfeeding - even if it's just morning and evening feeds - for up to two years will give your baby a great start in life. But you may feel that this is the right time to move on to bottle feeding expressed or formula milk. There are 'follow-on' milks available, but first stage baby milk is also suitable for the first 12 months. Be warned that if your baby has been purely breastfed until this stage, getting her to take a bottle may be a bit of a struggle. If there's a deadline looming, such as returning to work, it can easily become a stressful experience for both you and baby. Try to keep calm, and gently offer your baby a bottle instead of one of her usual breastfeeds.

You may like to try different styles of teats to see if there's one your baby prefers. Other tips include putting a little breastmilk on the teat so baby has a familiar smell and taste to start with. In most cases, your baby will adapt within a couple of days. Some breastfed babies refuse to take a bottle at all, and move straight from breastfeeding to sipping from a cup.

Good drinks

She's still too young for normal cow's milk as a main drink at six months, but it's safe to give her cooled, boiled water in addition to formula or breast milk, and well-diluted fruit juice with meals (one part juice to 10 parts water). Bear in mind that fruit juice contains natural sugars and is acidic, so too much can cause tooth decay and erosion over time. You can give drinks, including formula, in a lidded beaker or 'sippy' cup or, if you feel she's ready, introduce a double-handled cup and help her sip from it. A lidded cup is practical for giving drinks when you're out and about. Drinking from a cup gets more important as her teeth come through - sucking from a bottle exposes them to more sugar over a longer period. Be ready with a bib and a cloth as learning to drink from a cup is a messy business so is best done in a highchair and always under your supervision.

Ready to start weaning?

At around six months, your baby should be able to sit up, support her head, and reach for objects. At this stage, she'll love putting her toys in her mouth and chewing them. Another sign she's ready for solids is taking an interest in what you eat, trying to grab it and put it in her mouth. If you're not sure, try the banana test. Hold out a piece of banana - if your baby is able to grab it, put it in her mouth and eat some of it, she's ready for solids.

for babies

Baby's first foods

At the start of weaning, variety is more important than quantity. You're aiming to introduce your baby to a range of new flavours and textures, so don't worry about how much she's actually eating. It's an exciting time for your baby, and she's less likely to become a fussy eater if you allow her to explore a wide range of new foods, at her own pace. And it's worth remembering that babies can reject new foods up to 10 times before accepting them, so it's worth trying again with a refused food a few days later.

If you're breastfeeding, carry on with your normal feeds. Your baby will slowly reduce the amount of milk she wants as her intake of solid foods goes up. Supplementing with vitamin drops from six months onwards will ensure she gets enough of vitamins A, C and D for healthy growth and development. Always choose a supplement formulated for babies, such as the NHS Healthy Start vitamin drops, available free if you're eligible or from health clinics and GP's surgeries. Your baby won't need extra vitamins if she's having 500ml of formula or more a day, as vitamins and minerals are added to baby milk.

When starting out on their weaning adventure, many mums begin by offering a few teaspoons of baby rice mixed with a little of baby's normal milk at the lunchtime feed. But you could also try their milk mixed with some vegetables or fruit – try mashed potato, parsnip, avocado, cooked pear or apple. Your baby will be keen to touch the food and it's great to let her feed herself with her fingers as soon as she can (wash her hands first!). But when you're using a spoon, wait until she opens her mouth. (See below for more on spoon-feeding versus self-feeding.) After she's happily taking solids at lunchtime, you can introduce some foods at breakfast and after another few days, at tea-time too.

Purée-based weaning

Generations of babies have been weaned on purées, and this may be the approach you're happiest with. Making up a variety of purées can be a great way of exposing your baby to a wide variety of tastes, and you can also vary the texture to get her used to 'lumps'. And it should be easy enough to simply purée the suitable foods from your normal meal (minus the salt). By gradually introducing finger foods alongside purées, she'll also be learning to feed herself and chew.

We've divided purée feeding into three stages – Taste, Try and Texture. Your baby will only be used to milk, so the aim of the Taste stage is to give baby an ▶

MY STORY

'Theodore has become a lot more interested in what's on people's plates, and he'll watch you put food in your mouth. I was once holding him with an apple in the other hand, got distracted, and when I looked down he was licking the apple! That was pretty funny!'
Maria Onyango, Mum to Theodore, 5½ months

introduction to her first bland flavours. Purées at this stage should be simple, with mild flavours and smooth textures. By 7-9 months you can begin the Try stage and introduce a combination of different flavours. Move on to lumpier food to help with the process of learning to chew and swallow. By 9-12 months, your baby will be ready for the Texture stage. She should be eating three meals a day – all food should be chopped, mashed or minced, rather than puréed. You'll see all these stages in action in the recipes from p60.

Baby-led weaning

You may have come across the term 'baby-led' weaning – it's fast becoming a popular alternative to starting babies on purées. It's also known as 'self-feeding' and basically skips the purée stage altogether. So, instead of spoon-feeding your baby, you allow her to feed herself, with suitable foods she can grasp with her fingers, put into her mouth and chew. The theory is that this way, she's learning to chew right from the start – whereas with purées, all she needs to do to eat is swallow. Many mums say that self-feeding babies don't struggle with lumps as much as those who've been purée-fed. And, because she is self-feeding rather than being spoon fed, she can match her intake to her appetite.

Many mums try baby-led weaning with a second child, when there's less time available for mixing up purées. It probably won't suit you if you hate mess – a lot of the food will end up on the floor, walls, or in your baby's hair! But if this approach appeals, start by offering steamed and cooled carrots or broccoli, chunks of washed cucumber, or pieces of banana. All you have to do is simply place the food on the clean tray of her highchair. A lot of the food, especially initially, will come back out of her mouth which may make you wonder if she's getting enough to eat. However, at the early stages, her main nourishment will still be milk (breast or formula). And, as you will notice from her nappies, some food does go down!

After the initial few months – and once you've ruled out any reactions to foods (see Allergy Watch, right) – the aim is to give your baby manageable chunks of whatever the family is eating. It will mean adjusting your cooking style a little. For example, if you usually add salt – separate a portion for baby before adding seasoning to the meal.

Storing and reheating food

Cool cooked food as quickly as possible (within one to two hours) and put it in the fridge or freezer. Chilled baby food should be eaten within two days. Frozen food must be thoroughly defrosted before reheating. The safest way to do this is to leave it in the fridge overnight or use the defrost setting on a microwave.

Reheat food thoroughly so it is piping hot all the way through, but let it cool before giving it to your baby. If you need to cool food quickly, put it in an airtight container and hold under a cold running tap for a minute or so.

If using a microwave, always stir the food and check the temperature before feeding it to your child. Don't reheat cooked food more than once.

Allergy watch

Allergic diseases in children seem to be on the increase, although as yet, we don't know why. One theory is that our homes are much cleaner these days, so children don't get the exposure to germs they need for the normal development of their immune system. Food allergies in babies are most common if there's a family history of allergy, known as atopy, (including food allergies, eczema, hayfever and asthma), or if your baby suffers from eczema herself (especially if your baby's eczema is severe).

Which foods cause allergies?

Any food can potentially cause an allergic reaction in children, but the most common foods children are allergic to are peanuts, nuts, milk and eggs. Other allergens include sesame, fish, shellfish, celery, mustard, wheat, gluten, soya and foods containing sulphites (check food labels).

When should I introduce these foods?

There is no recommendation to avoid these foods during pregnancy or breastfeeding but the Department of Health currently recommends that none of the above foods be given to a baby under the age of six months. However, after six months, you can introduce these foods (to babies with a family history of allergy too), while keeping an eye out for allergies. This includes nut butters, such as peanut butter (though whole nuts shouldn't be given to children under five, because of the risk of choking).

It is understandable that if your family has a history of allergies, particularly allergies to nuts, you may be concerned about giving nut butters to your baby – discuss this with your dietitian or doctor.

When you start to introduce these allergenic foods, do so category by category, such as dairy then egg then wheat. Start with a small amount of a food only and introduce no more than one new allergenic food at a time, allowing at least three days between each new food group to give you enough time to spot any symptoms your child might show. By the age of 12 months, all the major high-risk foods should have been introduced.

What to look out for

The symptoms of food allergies are normally grouped according to the time it takes for the symptoms to appear following an allergenic food being eaten. Immediate type symptoms tend to appear within seconds to two hours of eating the food and can include lip swelling, itchiness, hives, rash, a red flushing of the face or body, worsening of eczema or breathing difficulties. If you think your baby is having an immediate allergic reaction, seek urgent medical advice (take your baby to your GP or, if necessary, to A&E) because in very rare cases, a severe reaction (anaphylaxis) can be life-threatening.

The more delayed type symptoms, often associated with allergy to cow's milk, include nausea, vomiting/reflux, diarrhoea, constipation, blood in stools, redness around the bottom, progressive worsening of eczema and, longer-term, problems with gaining weight. Some of the immediate and delayed type symptoms, like rashes and diarrhoea, are common symptoms of other illnesses too – consult a doctor if you are unsure. Your GP should be your first port of call if you suspect a food allergy and he or she will be able to advise you on allergy testing.

Remember that many children eventually outgrow their allergies so don't forget to speak with your GP about this too.

'There are a few simple precautions you can take to minimise the risk of choking'

My story

'If we tell our little Aaron that this cereal is what Daddy eats, then he's really keen. Add to that some encouraging "oohs" and "aahs" as we tip it in a bowl, and it goes down a treat!'

**Catherine Edwards,
Mum to Aaron, 2**

Choking risks

Choking in babies can be both frightening and dangerous. But a few simple precautions can minimise the risk. First, make sure she's sitting up straight when she eats, ideally in a highchair. It goes without saying that you should always be there when she eats, and she shouldn't be left unattended. Babies are most likely to choke on hard foods such as raw carrot sticks or chunks of apple, and small, round foods such as grapes or cherry tomatoes. Lightly cooking hard vegetables such as carrots can reduce the risk, and it's best to cut grapes and tomatoes in half. The skin from meat such as sausages, along with fish bones, can also be choking hazards, so take care to remove these before feeding them to your baby.

In most cases of choking, babies cough the food back up. But if she cannot cough or breathe, then lay her face down on your forearm, with her head lower than her body and her head and shoulders supported by the palm of your hand. Use the heel of your free hand to sharply slap the upper part of her back to try and dislodge the object. (For children under one, use the palms of your fingers to do this.) If this doesn't clear the obstruction, turn your baby over onto her back and push down with two fingers into the middle of her chest, three times. If this does not work, call 999 immediately, then continue to alternate back and front pressure until the ambulance arrives. Even if an ambulance is not required and the food is dislodged, seek medical attention to make sure all is well.

Q Our family is vegetarian. Should I do anything special when my baby is ready for solids?

A If you are following a vegetarian diet for your baby, it's important to make sure that it delivers all the nutrients she needs. A vegetarian weaning diet could provide fewer calories, less iron and more fibre, than one that includes meat and fish, so you need to address this by providing meat alternatives such as pulses, eggs or tofu. You should also provide fruit and vegetables alongside these, as the vitamin C they contain helps the body absorb iron. Too much fibre will fill up your baby too quickly without providing enough calories, so limit how much you give her. Vegan diets are not recommended for the weaning stage, but if you do decide to follow a vegan diet, you may need to give your baby supplements. You should talk to a healthcare professional about this. For more information about vegetarian and vegan diets for toddlers, see p94.

Foods to watch out for...

There are lots of foods your baby will love and which make fantastic weaning foods but here are a few you need to watch out for before giving to your little ones

Unpasteurised milk

Avoid unpasteurised milk products as these foods can contain bacteria that may cause food poisoning.

Honey

Do not give your baby honey or foods containing honey until they're at least 12 months. Although rare, honey can contain bacteria that can produce toxins in a baby's intestines, leading to a very serious illness (infant botulism). Also honey is a sugar, so avoiding it will also help prevent tooth decay.

Salt

Babies shouldn't eat much salt as their kidneys can't cope with it. Don't add salt to your baby's meals. Sainsbury's sell no-added salt stock and stock cubes for family cooking.

Raw shellfish

Don't give raw shellfish as it can contain harmful bacteria that may increase the risk of food poisoning in young children.

Mould ripened soft cheese

Avoid giving your baby mould ripened soft cheeses as these can contain bacteria that may cause food poisoning.

Sugar

Your baby doesn't need added sugar in her diet. By avoiding sugary snacks and drinks, you'll help prevent tooth decay. Use washed fruit or breast milk to sweeten food, if necessary.

Low-fat foods

Fat is an important source of calories and some fat-containing foods provide vitamins, such as vitamin A. It's better for babies and young children under two to have full-fat dairy products such as whole milk and full-fat yogurt and cheese rather than low-fat varieties.

Saturated fat

Don't give your older child too many foods that are high in saturated or 'bad' fat, such as biscuits, cakes, fatty sausages and burgers or chips. These are not appropriate weaning foods.

Nuts

Whole nuts, including peanuts, should not be given to children under five years old as they can choke on them. You can give your baby nut butters (eg peanut butter) from six months onwards, while keeping an eye out for signs of allergy (see p49).

Eggs

Make sure they're cooked until both the white and yolk are solid.

Shark, swordfish and marlin

Avoid these fish as they may contain higher levels of mercury that can affect a baby's developing nervous system.

Your weaning checklist

Making your own baby food is not difficult – you don't need complicated gadgets or to be an expert cook. However, it will be easier if you have some basic kit – you'll probably find you have most of these items in your kitchen already...

Sieve
A good old-fashioned sieve will come in handy, particularly if you're only making small quantities of food for baby, as it's quicker and easier to clean than a blender. It is especially good for sieving out fruit seeds and pips.

Chopping boards
Hygienic chopping boards are a must, so it's a good time to invest in some new ones, including a separate one for raw meat. If you want to follow best kitchen practice, get a complete set of colour-coded ones for chopping different foods – red for raw meat, blue for raw fish, yellow for cooked meat, green for salad and fruit, brown for vegetables and white for dairy and bread.

Steamer
The familiar folding metal steamers work really well (as do colanders) - just sit them over a pan of boiling water, add the veg and pop a lid over. If you like, you could invest in an electric steamer, which is useful if you're making large quantities.

Saucepans
A good quality, non-stick saucepan with a lid is a must for cooking up food for baby. It's also worth getting a small non-stick pan for heating up small amounts of food.

Blender
A blender is useful for making very smooth purées. You can choose either a jug-style blender with a lid, or a hand-held one that you use to blend food in a bowl. Buy the best one you can afford, as it's likely to get a lot of use.

Lindam mini blender

Vegetable peeler and kitchen knife
You'll be doing a lot of peeling and chopping, so if you don't already have a good-quality vegetable peeler and kitchen knife, buy them now!

Steriliser
When you first wean, you may want to sterilise food bowls and

Plastic containers
Ice cube trays are a handy way of portioning out purées – just pop out a cube to defrost when needed. Cool food before filling the trays, then wrap in clingfilm to avoid spillages. Otherwise, small sealable plastic containers are great. Freezer bags are also a good option for freezing individual portions for older toddlers.

Bibs

Let's be honest, feeding is messy, which means bibs are essential! You can buy cover-all bibs or bibs with curved rims to catch any missed mouthfuls - anything you can wipe-clean will do the job.

feeding equipment. You can do this by immersing them in boiling water for at least 5 minutes before use. You'll find it a lot easier if you get a steam steriliser or use your dishwasher on a hot wash cycle (80°C) - this is useful for larger items. Many mums stop sterilising after the first few weeks. You should always sterilise bottles and teats.

Labels and marker pen
Purées have a tendency to look pretty much the same, only in slightly different colour variations. That's why it's a good idea to label them before putting them in the freezer. Include the date you've made the food, so you know when to use it by.

Mess mats
Feeding time often ends up with more food on the floor than in baby's tummy, so a mess mat to pop under the highchair is a wise idea. Although a purpose-bought plastic mat is ideal, you can avoid shelling out extra cash by using an old towel or sheet instead.

Face cloths or muslins
Something to wipe mucky hands and faces with is a must. A face cloth or muslin - if only to lie on your lap to protect you from the flying debris - will do the job with, hopefully, minimum fuss from junior.

Beakers and cups
Meal-times are a good time to introduce beakers and cups. Again, you'll find them in all sizes and designs so there may be an element of trying out a few before you find one that works best for your baby. You'll need two or three.

Highchair
You'll be so spoilt for choice when it comes to buying a highchair that your biggest headache will be which one to choose. It's worth considering whether the chair is easy to fold and store away, how easy it is to clean, if the tray is removable for washing and whether you can adjust the height for your growing baby.

Bowls
You'll probably need 3 or 4 plastic weaning bowls for serving up baby food - and one should be a travel bowl with a lid and spoon for when you're on the move. Bowls come in all shapes and sizes - you can buy bowls with compartments for a variety of foods, handles for better grip and suction pads so your little one can't chuck her tea all over the kitchen floor!

Spoons

You'll need a good supply of plastic weaning spoons. You'll probably try a few different shaped spoons before you find the one that suits you and your little one best. Look out for heat-sensing spoons, which change colour when baby's food is too hot.

The essential weaning food guide

Here's a comprehensive rundown of what foods to introduce to your baby and when is the best time to give them

	First foods	6-7 months	7-9 months	9-12 months	12 months +
Meals per day	If you decide to wean before 6 months, talk to your health visitor or GP about what foods are best to give. Don't start weaning before 17 weeks. If you're weaning after 17 weeks; try 1 meal per day at 4-5 months, moving on to 2 after 2-3 weeks. Introduce a third at 5-6 months	2 or 3 small meals	3 small meals	3 main meals, plus 1 or 2 healthy snacks (see p150-159 for ideas)	3 main meals, plus 1 or 2 healthy snacks (see p150-159 for ideas)
Texture of food (purée-based weaning)	Very smooth, fine purée	Smooth purée, thicker consistency	Lumpier purée – add a few herbs and spices to broaden the palate. Soft finger foods can also be introduced*	Coarsely mashed, minced or chopped. Introduce more cooked and also raw finger foods	Chopped or cut into small pieces
Veg/fruits	Simple fruit and vegetable purées such as cooked apple or pear, potato, squash, parsnip, sweet potato and carrot	Introduce raw ripe fruit and veg such as banana, pear, mango and avocado. Purée cooked veg such as carrot, swede, broccoli, courgettes, cauliflower and parsnips. Try cooked fruit such as red berries, rhubarb and plums (stones removed)	Introduce finger foods such as cooked carrots, green beans and broccoli florets, raw cucumber sticks. Try strawberries, raisins, halved grapes and tomatoes, melon slices as fruity finger foods. Introduce stronger flavoured veg such as onions, leeks and mushrooms, spinach, peppers and higher-fibre veg, such as sweetcorn or peas	Introduce a wider range of vegetables and lightly cooked finger foods such as parsnip and broccoli, and soft foods such as avocado slices. You can also start to offer raw finger food (such as carrots) and a wider, more exotic choice of fruit such as papaya and kiwi as well as dried apricots, figs or prunes	As 9-12 months
Grains/pulses	Baby rice (sugar-free), cornmeal, millet, ground sago or tapioca, mixed with water, breast milk or formula milk	Red lentils, puréed with veg; introduce gluten-containing grains such as wheat, barley and oats but keep portions small. Try cooked pasta pieces as finger food	Try pasta, oats, adding flour in cooking, couscous, semolina, wheat and barley. You can include more types of lentils and soaked cooked dried beans and chickpeas	Introduce more grains but limit quantities of high-fibre wholegrains. Continue to give beans and pulses	As 9-12 months
Dairy	No† (other than cow's milk based infant formula)	Full-fat yogurt, fromage frais or custard (choose low-sugar varieties or make your own)	Try cow's milk in cooking and cheese that's low in salt	You can increase amounts of dairy, but continue to avoid mould ripened cheeses and unpasteurised milk products until your baby is a year old	As 9-12 months

* Soft finger foods can be introduced from weaning for baby-led weaning

	First foods	6-7 months	7-9 months	9-12 months	12 months +
Fish	No†	White fish with bones carefully removed. Purée steamed fish with vegetables	Introduce tiny portions of oily fish such as salmon and mackerel, or canned tuna (not in brine), with bones removed	Give white fish at least once a week, and up to 2 portions of oily fish	As 9-12 months
Meat	Puréed, well-cooked poultry and lean red meat	As first foods	Try a wider variety of meats and cuts	Increase amount and variety – can offer small amount of well-cooked liver once a week. Only give very small portions of salty meats, such as ham	As 9-12 months
Eggs	No†	Well-cooked eggs, finely chopped	Well-cooked eggs, finely chopped	Well-cooked, chopped eggs	Well-cooked, chopped eggs
Nut/seeds	No†	Ground nuts, seeds and peanut butter (See p49 if you have allergy concerns.) Avoid whole nuts as they can cause choking	As 6-7 months	As 6-7 months	As 6-7 months
Milk drinks	Breast feeds or at least 500ml follow-on formula milk. No cow's, goat's or sheep's milk as a main drink until 12 months	As first foods	As first foods	As first foods	Breast feeds or 300ml follow on formula milk or full-fat (whole) cow's milk
Other drinks	Cooled boiled water	Cooled boiled water	Tap water	Tap water; diluted fruit juice (one part juice to 10 parts water)	As 9-12 months
Foods to avoid	Salt, honey, unpasteurised milk products, mould ripened soft cheeses, low-fat foods, whole nuts and seeds, and very strong spices/flavours. Potentially allergenic foods†: Cereals containing wheat or gluten (eg bread, flour, pasta, rusks and oats), eggs, cows' milk (other than formula milk) and dairy foods, soya-based products, fish and shellfish, nuts and sesame	Salt, honey, unpasteurised milk products, mould ripened soft cheeses, whole nuts and low-fat foods	As 6-7 months	As 6-7 months	Low fat foods and whole nuts. Note, after 12 months honey is safe to give to your child
Portion size These are rough amounts - be guided by your baby's appetite	1-3 tsp per meal	2-3 tbsp per meal	3-4 tbsp per meal	3-6 tbsp per meal	6-10 tbsp per meal

† For advice on introducing potentially allergenic foods before 6 months, speak to your health visitor, dietitian or doctor.

" I can't wait until Ollie's talking and playing in the garden. If weaning is anything to go by, we're in for a fun ride! "

Michael Luck,
Dad to Ollie, 6 months

Purée-based weaning

Perfect
purées

Choosing purée-based weaning means your baby's first foods are likely to be vegetable or fruit-based purées. Cooking for your baby needn't be complicated, but there are a few rules to follow.

Your baby's immune system is still developing, so good hygiene will help to protect him from tummy upsets. Always wash your hands before preparing food and clean your baby's hands before he eats. You don't need to sterilise your baby's bowls or utensils, but they should be washed in hot, soapy water and rinsed thoroughly. Always use a clean knife and chopping board when preparing meals and wash and peel fruit and vegetables. See p6 for more hygiene and general safety advice.

Safe storage

Tempting as it may be, don't save unfinished meals to reheat later. Food that's been in contact with your baby's mouth or spoon could contain bacteria that may multiply during storage. But it is fine to refrigerate or freeze leftovers that haven't been given to your baby. Let food cool, then cover it and get it in the fridge or freezer within two hours (see p7 for more on storage, freezing and reheating). Any longer and bacteria could develop.

Small lidded pots can be handy, but freezing purée in ice cube trays is also a good idea, as you can pop out a cube or two as needed. As with a pot, cool the purée before filling the tray, then cover it with a freezer bag. Mark the date on the bag and use it within three months

or less according to the guidelines from your freezer manufacturer.

If you're giving food from a jar, put what you need into a clean bowl so you can refrigerate the food remaining in the jar. It'll be safe to use for up to 48 hours. If feeding directly from the jar, throw away leftover food, as it will have come into contact with bacteria from your baby's mouth.

Reheating stored food

The golden rules are don't reheat cooked food more than once, and when you do reheat, food should be piping hot all the way through. Allow it to cool, stir well, then taste to check the temperature before giving it to your baby. To cool food quickly, put it in a plastic container and run it under the cold tap. If using

MY STORY
'Bella kept picking at what we were eating so we knew she was ready for proper food, despite her having no teeth! The transition only took a week but it did get a bit messy – she just loved to fling it at the walls!'

Amy King, Mum to Bella, 7½ months

Food safety is simple if you bear these numbers in mind:

3 months
It's best to use frozen baby food within this time

2 days
Throw away baby food that's been stored in the fridge after this time

2 hours
This is your deadline to get cooked baby food into the fridge or freezer

MY STORY
'Moving from milk to purée was easier than I was expecting. There was a lot of mess to start with, but he enjoys the purées more than milk and I must say I quite like some of them myself!'

Mike Luck, Dad to Ollie, 6 months

Portion sizes
Your baby's stomach is about the size of his clenched fist, so he can comfortably eat a portion of food the same size. Start with a few teaspoons at a time and work up to two or three tablespoons per meal. Be led by his appetite – don't force him to finish each meal.

Food on the move
There's no doubt that shop-bought baby food is useful when you're on the move, but make sure you check the seals on cans, packets and jars are intact before use. Many babies are happy to eat these at room temperature, but they can also be warmed by standing in hot water.

If you prefer your baby to eat home-cooked meals, you can safely transport lidded pots of your own purée in an insulated cool bag with an ice pack. Just be sure to use them within four hours. Many restaurants and cafés will heat up baby food for you. If you don't have access to a microwave, try making a pot of banana or avocado purée. Finger food is also good when away from home if your baby has reached this stage. Try taking a lidded pot of steamed, cooled carrot sticks, chunks of washed cucumber or chopped strawberries. Other portable snack ideas include pots of baby yogurt, cooked cooled pasta shapes, rice cakes or oatcakes.

If you don't have an ice pack to place in a cool bag, take a pot of frozen food instead – it will be safe to eat within four hours of defrosting. But always heat thoroughly before serving.

food from the freezer, defrost in the fridge overnight, or use the defrost setting on your microwave. Again, heat it until it's piping hot, then allow to cool, stir and check before feeding it to your baby. Never refreeze food that's been previously frozen.

Getting started

Introducing your baby to new tastes is the first stage of purée-based weaning

Purée-based weaning is divided into three stages – taste, try and texture. Your baby will only be used to the taste and texture of milk, so the aim of the 'taste' stage is to gently introduce her to new flavours and a more solid texture. Purées in this stage should be very smooth and still quite liquid, with mild flavours.

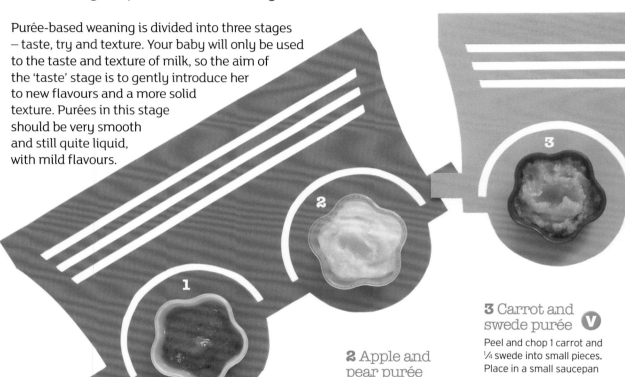

1 Rhubarb and strawberry purée

Roughly chop 4 rhubarb sticks and bake in the oven at 180°C, fan 160°C, gas 4 for 30 mins. Cool. Hull 200g washed strawberries and purée together with the rhubarb and the juice of 1 orange to the desired consistency.

2 Apple and pear purée

Peel, core and quarter 1 apple and 1 pear. Put in a small saucepan and just cover with boiling water. Simmer for 4-5 mins until the fruit has begun to soften. Drain and purée to the desired consistency.

3 Carrot and swede purée Ⓥ

Peel and chop 1 carrot and ¼ swede into small pieces. Place in a small saucepan and cover with cold water. Bring to the boil and simmer for 10-12 mins until tender. Drain and purée to the desired consistency.

4 Creamy broccoli purée V

Steam some broccoli florets for around 10 mins, or until tender. Purée to the desired consistency, adding a small amount of baby's usual milk to give it a creamy texture.

❄ All these purées are suitable for freezing, unless otherwise stated. See p7 for freezing advice.

5 Butternut squash and sage purée V

Preheat the oven to 220°C, fan 200°C, gas 7. Drizzle 1kg peeled, deseeded and chopped butternut squash with ½ tbsp olive oil and roast in the oven for 25 mins. Add 2-3 fresh sage leaves and roast for a further 5-10 mins until the butternut squash is tender. Purée to the desired consistency.

6 Parsnip and baby rice V

Peel 1 medium parsnip and cut into small pieces. Place in a small saucepan of boiling water and simmer until tender (about 6-8 mins). Drain and set aside. Make up baby rice by adding 2 tbsp baby's usual milk to 30g baby rice. Add it to the parsnip and purée to the desired consistency.

Adding flavours

In the second stage, you can start to try different flavour and texture combinations

By 7-9 months you can begin the 'try' stage and introduce dishes made up of a combination of different, stronger flavours from the main food groups (see weaning foods table on p54). Textures can be slightly firmer and lumpier now, to help with learning to chew.

1 Beetroot, apple and pear purée

Peel, trim and dice 300g beetroot and place in a saucepan with 300ml water. Cook, covered, for 15 mins. Meanwhile, peel, core and cut 450g Braeburn apples and 300g Sainsbury's Basics pears into pieces that are about the same size as the beetroot. Add to the pan. Cover and cook for a further 20 mins. Drain and purée to the desired consistency.

2 Leek, carrot and potato mash V

Bring a pan of water to the boil. Chop 1 peeled baking potato, 1 carrot and ½ leek and add to the pan. Cook for 20 mins, until tender. Drain the vegetables, then purée to the desired consistency with a little cream cheese.

3 Chicken, coriander and sweetcorn

Place 1 skinless, boneless chicken breast in a pan of boiling water, reduce to a simmer and poach for 10 mins. Remove and tear into shreds. Drain a 198g tin of no added salt sweetcorn kernels into a saucepan, add the chicken, 75ml water and a small handful of torn coriander leaves. Bring to a simmer, then purée to the desired consistency.

'Now's the time to introduce them to lots of new flavours!'

ANNIE DENNY, SAINSBURY'S NUTRITIONIST

4 Blueberry dream purée

Place 4 apples, each peeled and sliced, into a saucepan with 4 stoned, sliced plums. Add 5 tbsp apple juice and bring to a simmer. Cook for 10 mins, covered. Add 150g blueberries and cook for a further 5 mins. Purée to the desired consistency and serve on its own, or stir into porridge or yogurt.

5 Mango and berry purée

Peel and slice 1 ripe mango down either side of the stone and cut into chunks. Put the flesh into a bowl. Add a handful berries, such as strawberries and raspberries, and purée to the desired consistency. Add 1-2 tbsp yogurt, if you like.

6 Clementine and yogurt dessert

Put 4 whole peeled and deseeded clementines in a pan with 50ml apple juice. Cover and cook gently for 45 mins until softened. Cool and purée to the desired consistency with 100ml Greek yogurt. When making for older babies, freeze in ice lolly moulds.

7 Tomato and red pepper purée

In a small frying pan, heat a drizzle of olive oil. Add ½ small, chopped onion and 1 deseeded and diced red pepper. Lightly fry until softened (about 5 mins). Add 2 chopped tomatoes and 1 tsp tomato purée, then cover and cook for a further 4 mins. Purée to the desired consistency.

8 Celeriac and potato purée

Cook 250g peeled and diced potatoes and 250g diced celeriac in boiling water for 8-10 mins or until tender. Drain and purée to the desired consistency with 10g unsalted butter, 1 tbsp fresh chopped dill and 50-75ml whole milk.

9 No-cook cucumber and avocado purée

Peel 1 small cucumber, remove the seeds and roughly chop. Roughly chop ¼ ripe, peeled and stoned avocado. Purée to the desired consistency with the cucumber and 1 tbsp natural yogurt.
Not suitable for freezing.

10 Cheesy cauliflower and potato bake

Cook 250g cauliflower florets and 200g peeled, diced potatoes in a pan of water for 15-20 mins until soft, then drain. Melt 40g unsalted butter in a pan and cook 100g finely chopped leeks for 5 mins. Add 25g flour, cook for 1 min, remove from heat and whisk in 250ml whole milk. Return to heat and simmer for 2 mins. Stir in 30g grated mild Cheddar and the veg. Spoon into an ovenproof dish, sprinkle with 1 tbsp grated cheese and put under a preheated grill for 10 mins. Purée to the desired consistency .

11 Broccoli, pea and pear mash

Place 300g broccoli florets in a medium saucepan with 3 peeled and sliced pears. Add 250ml boiling water and cook, covered, over a medium heat for 20 mins, stirring occasionally. Add in 160g pack of Sainsbury's hand-shelled peas halfway through. Purée to the desired consistency.

12 Baby bubble and squeak

Bring a pan of water to the boil and add 350g Sainsbury's Basics potatoes, peeled and cut into small chunks. Cook for 25 mins, adding 250g peeled and diced carrots after 10 mins. Finely chop 200g cored green cabbage, add to the vegetables and cook for a further 5 mins. Drain well. Heat 30g unsalted butter in a frying pan and add the vegetables. Using a fork, mash the vegetables and mix together over a low heat for 5 mins, until it's the right consistency.

Learning to chew

Lumpier textures with bite-sized pieces in this stage help your baby master chewing

By 9-12 months, your baby is ready for the 'texture' stage. She should be eating three meals a day – all food should be chopped, mashed or minced, rather than puréed.

1 Sweetcorn, chicken and carrot purée

In a frying pan, heat a little olive oil over a low heat. Cut 150g chicken breast into small pieces, add to the pan and fry until cooked through. Add the kernels of 1 sweetcorn cob (or 120g tinned drained no added salt sweetcorn), 1 small grated carrot and 100ml low-salt vegetable stock to the pan. Simmer until the veg is tender. Mash or purée to the desired consistency.

2 Courgette, pea and mini pasta V

Cook 50g mini pasta shapes in a small saucepan of boiling water for 10 mins until tender. Meanwhile, in another pan, heat 1 tsp oil and add 40g grated courgette. Cook for a few mins, then add 50g peas, 2 chopped mint leaves and 30g ricotta. Drain the pasta, reserving 2-3 tbsp of the cooking water, and add the pasta and water to the veg. Mash to a rough purée. *Not suitable for freezing.*

3 Pollock and pea purée

Poach 100g pollock fillets in 200ml whole milk for 4-5 mins. Drain, reserving the milk. Meanwhile, cook 75g frozen peas, drain and mash. Flake the fish into the peas and stir in 50ml of the reserved milk. Mash or purée to the desired consistency. *Not suitable for freezing.*

4 Leek and pea risotto

Heat ½ tbsp olive oil in a pan, add 50g risotto rice and 1 thinly sliced leek, and cook over a low heat for 1 min. Gradually add 350ml hot, low-salt vegetable stock, stirring and allowing each addition to be absorbed before adding the next. Simmer until the stock is almost all absorbed, then stir in 50g frozen peas. Keep on the heat until all the stock is absorbed and the peas are cooked. *Not suitable for freezing.*

5 Chicken and asparagus purée

In a frying pan, heat 1 tsp olive oil and cook ½ roughly chopped onion until soft. Chop 150g chicken breast into small, bite-size chunks and add to the frying pan. Fry until golden. Turn down the heat and add 150g asparagus, trimmed into 2cm lengths. Cover and cook until soft – about 4 mins. Add 100ml soured cream to the pan and stir to warm through. Allow to cool slightly, then mash or purée to the desired consistency. If freezing, leave out the soured cream until reheating.

6 Avocado, cottage cheese and garlic purée

Mash ½ small, ripe, stoned avocado with 1 tbsp cottage cheese and ½ small crushed garlic clove. Thin with a little baby milk, if necessary. Eat this purée straight away. *Not suitable for freezing.*

7 Raspberry and orange summer pudding

Put 100g raspberries in a small saucepan, along with the zest of ½ orange and 2 tbsp freshly squeezed orange juice. Remove the crusts from 1 slice white bread, tear the slice into pieces and add to the pan. Heat gently for 5 mins until warmed through. Mash to a rough purée.

8 Berry rice pud

In a saucepan, bring 100g Sainsbury's pudding rice, 20g Sainsbury's Fairtrade light brown sugar and 375ml whole milk to a gentle simmer, stirring, for about 10-12 mins until the milk is almost all absorbed. Add a further 250ml whole milk and cook gently, until the rice is tender (about 6-8 mins). To serve, gently mash 50g fresh blackberries and 50g raspberries together and stir through the rice. **Not suitable for freezing.**

9 Bread and butter pudding

Preheat the oven to 180ºC, fan 160ºC, gas 4. Butter a 500ml shallow, heatproof pie dish. Remove the crusts from 5 slices of white bread, spread each slice with unsalted butter, then cut into 4 triangles. Arrange a layer of bread, buttered-side up, in the bottom of the dish, sprinkle over 35g raisins and a pinch of cinnamon, and cover with the remaining bread. Whisk 300ml whole milk with 2 eggs and 2 tbsp brown sugar. Pour the mixture over the bread, sprinkle over another 35g raisins and bake for 25 mins. Mash to a rough purée.

10 Courgette and baby spinach cheesy bake

Preheat the oven to 200°C, fan 180°C, gas 6. Slice 3 small courgettes and steam for 10-15 mins until soft. Place 200g washed baby spinach leaves in a pan, cover and cook for 3-4 mins. In another pan, mix 20g unsalted butter and 20g flour with 200ml milk. Heat, mixing with a whisk until the sauce bubbles for 1 min. Remove from the heat and stir in 70g grated Cheddar. Put the veg in an ovenproof dish and pour over the sauce. Sprinkle over a little more grated cheese and bake on the top shelf of the oven for 25 mins. Mash or purée to the desired consistency.

11 Haddock, sweetcorn and new potato supper

Heat 2 tsp oil in a pan, and cook 1 peeled and chopped onion with 1 chopped celery stick for 10 mins, covered. Add the kernels from 1 large sweetcorn to the pan, along with 200g potatoes, chopped into 2cm cubes, and 200ml whole milk. Cook for 10 mins. Add 200g skinless and boneless haddock loin (double check for any small bones), chopped into 4cm cubes, then cover and cook for 5 more mins. Mash or purée to the desired consistency.

12 Swede, sprouts and pork purée

In a deep frying pan, heat 1 tbsp olive oil and cook 1 small finely chopped onion for 5 mins to soften. Add 300g finely diced pork shoulder and cook for a further 5 mins. Add 300g swede, peeled and cut into small chunks, along with 250ml apple juice, 150g Brussels sprouts and 150ml low-salt vegetable stock. Cover and cook gently for 50 mins or until the meat and vegetables are tender. Mash or purée to the desired consistency.

' Letting Carrie feed herself is a real adventure — we've had the kitchen covered in all sorts! '

**Katie Millan,
Mum to Carrie, 12 months**

Finger food

Look mum, I'm feeding myself!

MY STORY

'Having tried various methods of feeding, the easiest seems to be just letting her get on with it herself. She tends to eat better than when I try to feed her.'

Jade Walkley, Mum to Bobbi, 18 months

When your baby is happily eating fruit- and veg-based purées, you can start to introduce finger foods. However, if you've opted for baby-led weaning (see p48 for more on this), you'll be introducing these foods from six months on.

You may start wondering whether finger foods are worth bothering with at first when most end up on the floor! But do persevere; encouraging your baby to chew is important as it strengthens jaw muscles, which can help with speech development. Finger foods also encourage babies to feed themselves, giving them a sense of control and independence. Finger

foods make good snacks on the go, but you can also offer them alongside their regular purées.

The usual allergy rules apply (see p49) – don't introduce more than one new food every three days, so you have time to monitor any symptoms. To prevent choking, give finger foods when they're sitting upright. And it goes without saying that you should never leave baby unsupervised with food.

It's best not to give your baby biscuits or too many other sweet foods at this stage – they don't offer much nutritionally, and developing a taste for sweet foods early on may make your baby more likely to reject savoury or more bland tastes.

Emotional eating

For most of us, food is tied up with emotion. As children we may have been told to eat everything on our plates, whether we felt hungry or not. As an adult, eating can be a source of comfort, a way of celebrating or a response to stress or boredom. Cooking and sharing food is often an expression of love in families.

So it's no surprise that weaning your baby can produce a roller coaster of emotions – from the delight of watching your baby happily tucking in to a meal, to the stress of desperately encouraging her to have 'just one more' mouthful.

It's easier said than done, but making mealtimes as relaxed as possible is the best approach you can take at this stage, for both you and your baby. Lots of smiles and attention around the table will make sure your baby associates eating with enjoyment and positivity.

Dealing with rejection
Refusing to try a new food doesn't mean your baby is turning into a fussy eater. It's normal for a baby to refuse a new food up to 10 times before it feels familiar enough for her to accept it.

Give your baby lots of encouragement when she eats well or tries a new food. Don't make a big fuss if she's reluctant to eat – the extra attention may inadvertently reinforce the behaviour. Simply take the food away, and try again at the next meal. And remember, it's normal for a baby to have a reduced appetite if she's feeling unwell or tired, or is distracted or teething.

Appetites can vary from day-to-day, so try not to get too hung up with what she eats on any one day. What your baby eats over the course of a week is more important. And every baby is different, so don't worry if other babies seem to be 'better' eaters! As long as your baby is gaining weight, and your doctor or health visitor has no concerns, then trust your baby's appetite. By not forcing her to eat when she's not hungry, she's less likely to get into the habit of overeating when she's older.

For more on fussy eaters, turn to p95.

MY STORY
'Feeding Carrie is always an experience – the kitchen gets so messy! But nothing is refused; she loves everything. Last week she even tried a tiny piece of smoked salmon for the first time!'
Katie Millan, Mum to Carrie, 12 months

Good foods for little hands

1. Chunks of banana
2. **Lightly buttered toast 'soldiers'**
3. Chunks of peeled apple or pear
4. **Strips of well-cooked omelette**
5. **Halved strawberries or halved grapes**
6. Cooked pasta shapes
7. **Strips of well-cooked chicken, lamb or beef**
8. **Chunks of cooked fish** (check for bones)
9. Chopped hard-boiled egg
10. Steamed pieces of veg (carrot batons, broccoli florets, chunks of sweet potato or butternut squash)

Spinach, tomato and potato croquettes Ⓥ

These tasty little savoury croquettes made with mashed potato
are really easy for youngsters to grab hold of and eat

500g potatoes,
roughly chopped
200g pack Sainsbury's
young leaf spinach, washed
25g plain flour, plus a little
extra for dusting
25g Sainsbury's sundried
tomatoes, finely chopped
75g Sainsbury's mild
British Cheddar, grated
1 free-range egg, beaten
80g fresh breadcrumbs
2 tbsp olive oil

1 Cook the potatoes in a pan of boiling water
until tender. Drain and mash, then set aside
in a large bowl.
2 Meanwhile, put the spinach in a colander and
pour boiling water over the leaves to wilt. Cool,
then squeeze out all the moisture and chop.
3 Add the flour, sundried tomatoes and Cheddar
to the potatoes. Mix well, then stir in the spinach.
4 Divide the mixture into 12 balls, then roll each
into a cylinder. Roll in the extra flour, dip in the
beaten egg, then coat in the breadcrumbs. Chill in
the fridge for 15 mins.
5 Heat the oil in a frying pan and fry each
croquette until golden all over. Serve with mini
plum tomatoes and blanched mange tout.

Tip...
These croquettes
can be served either
warm or cold and will
keep for up to 2 days
in the fridge.

SERVES 1 TODDLER
PREP TIME: 5 MINS
COOK TIME: 10-15 MINS

Poached chicken with steamed broccoli

Broccoli provides vitamin C, and the colourful florets
help to make this meal more appealing for little ones

2 Sainsbury's SO organic
free-range chicken
mini fillets or
mini chicken fillets
3-4 broccoli florets

1 Add the chicken fillets to a small pan of boiling
water, then bring up to the boil for 1 min. Turn off the
heat and leave, covered, for 10-15 mins. When the
chicken is cooked, remove from the pan and slice.
2 Meanwhile, bring another pan of water to the boil
and steam the broccoli florets until tender but not
too soft - about 4 mins depending on their size.
3 When cool enough to handle, serve the broccoli
florets with the chicken slices.

Jersey Royals, olives & sugar snaps Ⓥ

Kids love the taste of olives but only give them sparingly as they are high in salt
SERVES 2-4 TODDLERS. PREP TIME: 5-10 MINS. COOK TIME: 10-15 MINS

Cook 500g Jersey Royals in boiling water until tender, then drain and slice into
cubes. Cook 75g sugar snap peas in boiling water until tender, halve and toss
together with the potatoes, 50g pitted and halved black olives and 1 tbsp olive oil.

*Jersey Royals, olives &
sugar snaps*

Peanut butter triangles with melon

Peanut butter provides protein
and kids really love the taste!

2 tsp Sainsbury's
SO organic smooth
peanut butter
1 slice Sainsbury's
wholemeal bread
Charentais melon or melon
of your choice, to serve

1 Spread the peanut butter onto the
bread and cut into triangles.
2 Cut a wedge from a Charentais melon or
your choice of melon, then cut it into
chunks and serve alongside the bread.

**See p49 for information about
children and peanut allergies**

SERVES 2 TODDLERS.
PREP TIME: 5-10 MINS
COOK TIME: 25 MINS

Cheesy sweet potato wedges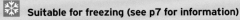

Little ones love sweet potatoes and these wedges are easy for small hands to pick up and eat

½ large or 1 medium
sweet potato, cut
into wedges
2 tsp vegetable or
olive oil
2 tsp grated Sainsbury's
Swiss Gruyère
or Cheddar cheese

1 Preheat the oven to 200ºC, fan 180ºC, gas 6. Put the potato wedges into a roasting dish with the oil and mix together to coat.
2 Roast for 20 mins, then move the wedges around in the dish and sprinkle the cheese over the top and roast for another 5 mins. Serve with a steamed green vegetable of your choice.

❄ **Suitable for freezing (see p7 for information)**

Boiled egg, broccoli and tomatoes Ⓥ

Plenty of colourful variety helps to get your little ones interested in their meal

1 egg

2 broccoli florets

1 tsp butter

1 slice white bread, toasted, crusts trimmed and cut into fingers

2 cherry tomatoes, halved

1 Bring a small saucepan of water to the boil. Add the egg and the broccoli. Remove the broccoli after 2 mins and leave to cool.

2 Continue boiling the egg for a further 8 mins. Drain the egg and run under cold water to cool before peeling and slicing into quarters.

3 Butter the toast fingers and serve with the bite-size pieces of broccoli, halved cherry tomatoes and quartered hard-boiled egg.

Katie says: *'This recipe went down really well with Carrie. It was so easy to make and all the different textures and tastes made it fun and interesting for her to eat.'*

SERVES 3 TODDLERS
PREP TIME: 10-15 MINS
COOK TIME: 35-40 MINS

Cheesy potato tortilla Ⓥ

Adding cheese to this tortilla is a good way to get some
extra calcium in their diet

300g new potatoes,
peeled and thinly sliced
1 tsp olive oil
1 small onion, finely sliced
3 free-range eggs,
lightly beaten
50g Sainsbury's mild
British Cheddar, grated

1 Put the potato slices in a pan of cold water, bring
to the boil, then simmer for 12 mins. Drain, tip into
a bowl and set aside.
2 Heat the oil in a 20cm ovenproof frying pan,
then add the onion and cook for 5 mins until
soft. Add to the bowl of potatoes, along with the
eggs and Cheddar. Stir to combine.
3 Preheat the grill to medium. Pour the potato
mixture back into the frying pan and cook over
a gentle heat on the hob for 15 mins until almost
cooked through. Place the pan under the grill for
5 mins until set and golden on top.
4 Leave to cool, then cut into fingers. Serve with
cherry tomato halves and cucumber batons.

'To avoid any chance of upset tummies, always
make sure eggs are well cooked for children'

JUSTINE REDFEARN, SAINSBURY'S FOOD SAFETY TEAM

MAKES 1 LOAF (10 SLICES)
PREP TIME: 15 MINS
COOK TIME: 50-55 MINS

Deliciously easy banana loaf

A lovely treat that's packed with banana flavour and goodness. This freezes well – wrapped in greaseproof paper and clingfilm or in freezer bags. Defrost thoroughly and serve at room temperature

80g butter, softened, plus extra for greasing

3 large or 4 medium really ripe bananas

1 tsp Sainsbury's Taste the Difference Madagascan vanilla extract

180g Sainsbury's light soft brown sugar or light muscovado sugar

1 free-range egg, beaten

225g self-raising flour

1 tsp baking powder

1 Preheat the oven to 180°C, fan 160°C, gas 4. Grease a 900g loaf tin with butter and line the base with greaseproof paper.

2 Break the bananas into pieces, put into a big bowl and mash with a potato masher. Add the 80g softened butter and vanilla extract, and mash again. The mixture will look lumpy.

3 Add the sugar and egg, and mix with a wooden spoon. Sift in the flour and baking powder, mix, then spoon into the prepared tin.

4 Bake for 40 mins, then remove from the oven. If the cake is browning too much, cover with greaseproof paper and bake for another 10-15 mins. To test if it is cooked through, insert a skewer into the centre – if it comes out clean the cake is cooked. Cut into slices to serve.

 Suitable for freezing (see p7 for information)

Tuna and sweetcorn mini finger sandwiches

If you haven't had time to make tea, try this super-fast idea using ingredients from your storecupboard and fridge

200g tin tuna in
spring water, drained
1 tbsp Sainsbury's
crème fraîche or
mayonnaise
198g tin sweetcorn
in water, drained
10g unsalted butter,
softened
4 slices brown bread

1 In a small bowl, combine the tuna, crème fraîche and sweetcorn. Season with a little black pepper.
2 Butter each slice of bread, then divide the tuna mixture between two slices. Top with the other two pieces of bread to make sandwiches.
3 To serve, cut off the crusts and cut into fingers. Arrange on a plate along with the cucumber and carrot batons. Tea in an instant!

Toasted brown bread squares with banana and honey

Use maple syrup instead of honey for toddlers under 1 year (see p51).
SERVES 1 TODDLER. PREP TIME: 5 MINS
Toast 1 slice of brown bread, then cut into squares. Top with slices of banana and drizzle with 1 tbsp honey or maple syrup.

Toasted brown bread squares with banana and honey

' Angelo loves the independence of feeding himself — there's nothing he can't tackle with his little knife and fork! '

Owen Blagrove, Dad to Angelo, 3

Beyond the first year

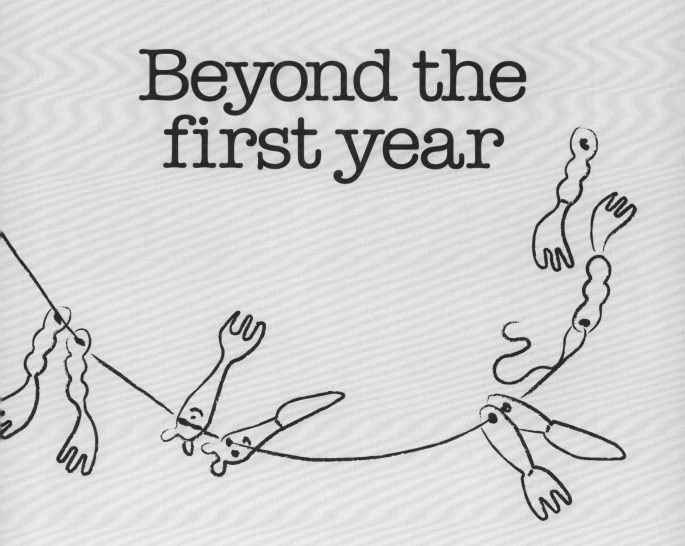

Feeding after the first year

Baby's first birthday is a big milestone for all the family. You've come a long way! Every child is different, but he's probably more active than he's ever been – he's mastered crawling and can whizz around the room at an amazing speed. He may love pulling himself up and 'cruising' the room, holding onto the furniture. Some babies will also have started walking. It can seem like he's learning new things every day at this stage – trying first words, clapping along with songs and joining in with actions. All that activity requires a lot of energy and nutrients, so a good diet is crucial.

Until 12 months, breast or formula milk has been his main source of nourishment, but now it's time for solid food to take centre stage! From this age and beyond, your aim is to introduce as many different foods as possible. Milk intake (see left) tends to drop off naturally as his intake of solids goes up, and from 12 months onwards it's fine to switch to whole cow's milk instead of formula. If you can, gradually phase out bottles and replace them with a beaker, which is better for his teeth. But be prepared; there can be a lot of comfort associated with a bottle, so he may be keen to hang onto his last bottle before bed in particular. If so, be sure to brush his teeth before he goes to sleep.

Try to include some starch, protein and fresh fruits or vegetables with every meal (see right). Keep introducing new foods, and remember he may need to try it up to 10 times before he decides he likes it! But be sure not to overload his plate – children can be daunted by big portions of food. Small portions of different foods arranged on a plate can be very appealing – make it into a smiley face if it helps! He can always have seconds if he's still hungry. Cutting up tricky foods such as meat or spaghetti will help him to feed himself.

How much milk?

Milk is an important source of calcium and other nutrients and, as well as water, should be the main drink for toddlers. One to five year olds need three daily servings of dairy, but vary these. As well as milk, give them cheese, yogurt or fromage frais. A serving is 150ml milk, a small pot of yogurt or a matchbox size piece of cheese. Give whole milk until they're two; after that you can give them semi-skimmed, if you like.

Children can be daunted by big portions of food

✔ GOOD FOODS FOR GROWING KIDS!

Full-fat dairy products.
Unless they have a dairy allergy, children can drink whole cow's milk from 12 months. Milk is a good source of calcium for growing bones. Give full-fat versions of dairy foods, such as yogurt and cheese, as these will contribute towards his energy and vitamin needs. Aim to include dairy products in three meals or snacks a day. Try macaroni cheese or rice pudding (see our recipes on p106 and p103), or cheese with an apple as a snack.

Starchy foods, such as bread, cereals, porridge, potatoes, rice, couscous or pasta provide energy, nutrients and some fibre. Starchy foods should make up half of each meal at this stage, with the other half divided between protein (meat, fish, eggs or beans) and fresh veg or fruit. White bread, rice and pasta are best as too many wholegrains may fill him up before he's got enough nutrients. But some wholegrains at this stage can help him get used to the taste. How about making sandwiches with one slice of white and one slice of brown bread? Baked and mashed potatoes are popular starch choices, or try mixing cooked rice or pasta with chopped veg and tinned tomatoes.

Foods containing protein provide the amino acids, iron and zinc he needs to grow. Toddlers and pre-schoolers need a portion of meat, fish or eggs at least twice a day. Vegetarian options include lentils and beans (including baked beans), nut butters, houmous, soya and tofu. If feeding a child a vegan diet, get advice from a paediatric dietitian (ask your GP for a referral). See p94 for more on vegetarian and vegan diets.

Milk and water should be his main drinks. Keep fruit juice well-diluted and at meal-times only, and limit or avoid fizzy drinks, due to their high sugar content.

Fresh fruit and veg for fibre, vitamins and antioxidants. Aim for 5-a-day and lots of variety – different coloured fruits and vegetables have different phytonutrients – nutrients from plants necessary for optimal health. Many kids prefer batons of raw veg such as cucumbers, carrots and peppers, rather than cooked. Frozen and tinned count towards your 5-a-day too.

✘ FOODS TO KEEP TO A MINIMUM

Salty foods
Crisps, processed meats (see below), pre-prepared sauces and some snack foods can be high in salt. Too much salt can put pressure on children's kidneys and cause dehydration. For children aged one to three, the recommended maximum amount is 2g of salt a day, and for children aged four to six, it is 3g of salt a day, so be sure to read food labels.

Sugary treats
Giving sweets, biscuits and cakes too frequently will encourage a sweet tooth and can contribute to tooth decay. It's tempting to use dessert as a reward for finishing his main course, but by doing so, you're sending a 'savoury food is bad, sweet food is good' message. Also, if you don't offer dessert after every meal, he won't get used to finishing his meal with a sweet taste. If you are giving treats, look for recipes for reduced-sugar versions of favourites like flapjacks or carrot cake to make at home, or try baked or fresh fruit with natural yogurt.

When checking food labels, be aware that these ingredients all contain sugars: invert sugar or syrup, honey, raw sugar, brown sugar, cane sugar, muscovado sugar, concentrated fruit juices, sucrose, glucose, dextrose, maltose, fructose and hydrolysed starch. Some breakfast cereals can be high in sugar – try porridge made with milk or water instead. Children respond to routine and they soon get used to rules that are stuck to consistently. If you want to give sweets, try choosing one day a week as 'sweetie day', when you go along to a sweet shop and he gets to choose from the toddler-friendly shelf. This can be a great defence against pester power later on ('no, we won't buy those sweets because it's not sweetie day...')!

Processed meats
Ham can seem like an easy thing to include in a sandwich. But the World Cancer Research Fund has advised that consumption of processed meats such as ham, salami, pastrami, hot dogs and bacon be kept to a minimum as they have been linked to an increased risk of cancer in later life. Try chicken breast, tinned salmon (checked for bones), soft cheese or sliced banana in sandwiches instead.

Lots of positive praise and attention is the best way to encourage learning

MY STORY

'It's all about experimenting with different foods – if I cook mixed veg bhajis, my little one eats veg that she usually refuses! I try not to put any pressure on her – instead I just ask her to show me her big, strong muscles!'

**Sunita Parmar,
Mum to Lilly, 3½**

Watching weight

Sadly, obesity in children is on the increase. From the national child measurement scheme introduced in 2006, which weighs children when they start and leave primary school, we now know that one in four five year olds is overweight. Plus, 16 per cent of children aged two to 15 are classified as obese, a figure that has increased by a startling 11 per cent in the past decade.

Needless to say, children should never be put 'on a diet', unless advised to do so by a health professional. But it's never too early to help them eat healthily. Being overweight as a child puts them at increased risk of asthma and diabetes, and research shows that eight out of 10 overweight children become overweight adults, reducing life expectancy by 14 years.

Portion control

Giving your child the right sized portions is important. For young toddlers, his stomach is roughly the same size as his clenched fist. As he becomes more active from two up, try gradually increasing the portions - be guided by his appetite and whether he asks for more when he's finished. As children reach school age, their appetites and calorie needs vary, depending on how naturally active they are and how fast they're growing. Unless your child is underweight, or losing weight, allow him to regulate his own food intake by stopping eating when he is full, rather than clearing his plate. Offer small meals with the option of seconds if he's still hungry, rather than overloading his plate. In addition to three nutritious meals, offer one healthy snack between each meal, opting for fruit, oatcakes, or a small yogurt rather than biscuits or crisps.

Don't forget that a child learns from his parents all the time, so seeing you eat chunks of apple or carrot sticks and houmous instead of a biscuit makes it more

Developing good habits

Routine is reassuring when you're a child. Habits such as washing hands before a meal and eating at a table without toys or TV, help signal 'meal-time' and encourage him to eat. Eating together as a family, is also important. Interacting with him during meals will help him associate them with pleasure.

TABLE MANNERS!

He's mastered finger foods, and from 13 months onwards, he may be ready to start using a spoon. But don't worry if he doesn't seem interested – some babies can't wait to feed themselves, others would be happily spoonfed until they start school!

Most babies have the necessary grip and co-ordination to use cutlery from around 13 months onwards, so encourage your little one to get the hang of a spoon at that age. Many children have mastered a knife and fork by the time they are three, but it may take others until they're five. As anyone who has more than one child will tell you, children develop at different rates! Children who were born prematurely for instance, often take longer to reach their milestones. If you have any concerns about your little one's progress, talk about it with your GP or health visitor.

Eating together as a family is the best way to encourage him to use a knife and fork. You can buy inexpensive sets of cutlery that are specially designed to fit little fingers. Try starting with a spoon first, then introducing a fork and, finally, swapping the spoon for a knife.

Child-size unbreakable plates or bowls are also invaluable – they'll help you serve the right portions and you won't have to worry when they get knocked onto the floor. A booster seat can also be a good investment. Attached to a chair, it takes up less space than a high chair and allows your child to eat at the table with the rest of the family. Opt for one with straps – great for safety and keeping a lively child in one place long enough to eat!

appealing for him. If you find it hard not to give in to requests for sweets and crisps between meals, not keeping them in the house can take that pressure off. Getting all family members on board is also important – grandparents can be the worst offenders in giving children 'treats'! It's natural they want to show their love, but perhaps you could gently suggest other ways to do this, such as giving stickers.

Staying active is also important, so when you're in a safe place, let him get out of his buggy. Pushing a doll's buggy or scooting along on a tricycle can encourage reluctant walkers. If you can, schedule at least an hour's active time each day such as a trip to a playpark, a swimming group or a game of football in the garden. If it's raining, try simply putting some music on and dancing together. If you do have concerns that your child is gaining too much weight, speak to your GP. He may refer you to a paediatric dietitian or healthy eating group for children.

The right rewards

When he's mastered a milestone, whether it's saying 'mama!', taking his first steps, or fitting puzzle pieces into the right shapes, your instinct will be to reward him. You're right – lots of positive praise and attention is the best way to encourage learning. But it's best not to get into the habit of rewarding achievements with a biscuit or ice-cream – brightly coloured stickers are a surprisingly successful alternative! At this stage, you're laying the foundations of habits that will last for the ▶

What about veggies and vegans?

If you're giving your toddler a vegetarian or vegan diet, you need to ensure he is getting the right nutrients and calories.

- Include iron-rich foods such as pulses, green veg, fortified cereals (choose low salt, low sugar varieties), cooked egg yolks and dried fruits. Vitamin C helps the body absorb iron, so include fruit, veg or juice with meals.
- Protein is found in pulses, eggs and dairy products, tofu, grains (eg bread) and nut butters (do not give children under five whole nuts). Some products, such as tofu and meat substitutes do contain protein, but are high in fibre and low in calories, so don't give too much of these to young children.
- Before giving toddlers food such as veggie sausages or burgers, check to see how much salt they contain.
- If you're giving your child a diet that doesn't contain dairy products or eggs, he may need supplements (such as Healthy Start vitamins and minerals, see below) or fortified products to ensure he gets the nutrients he needs, especially iron, calcium and vitamins D and B12. A paediatric dietitian can help with your toddler's needs.

MY STORY

'Angelo started using a knife and fork at the age of two. He would copy me at the dinner table and always tried to take my knfe and fork instead of using his spoon. He's now an expert at cutting up his own food!'

**Owen Blagrove,
Dad to Angelo, age 3**

rest of his life. A snack that's high in fat or sugar might put a smile on his face for a few minutes but encouraging healthy eating habits will make him happier in the long run. And try not to reach for the biscuit jar when he's fallen over or is upset. Toddlers are quick on the uptake - if he knows he gets a treat when cries, he'll soon learn to turn on whines and grumbles at will! Comfort him with a hug instead.

Happy eaters

Even enthusiastic eaters can become more picky at around the age of two or hree. It can be so frustrating when your child starts refusing foods he used to love! The good news is that it tends to be a phase. Try not to make meal-times a battleground; his total intake over a week is what counts.

If there are only one or two vegetables your child will eat, make sure he gets them every day. Continue to encourage him to taste new foods but if he refuses, don't push it. Many parents try subterfuge at this stage, 'hiding' vegetables by including them in a tomato-based sauce then puréeing it. It's easy to get into a routine based on the few meals

he willingly eats, but experimenting with new foods can produce surprising results - he might refuse mashed potato but love egg-fried rice! Don't rush meals - many children are slow eaters at this stage but if your little one has been sitting in his chair for 20 minutes or more and isn't making any progress, then he isn't going to eat any more. Growing veg in the garden is another really good way of engaging little ones with their food - kids love the idea of eating something they've helped to grow (see p164). See right for more ideas for tackling fussy eaters.

A little extra

If your child has been having Healthy Start vitamins (see p47) or another age-specific vitamin and mineral supplement, he can continue to have these up until the age of five. These vitamins will ensure he's getting enough vitamin D for healthy bones, as well as iron that can help safeguard against anaemia, which may affect his development.

How to tackle a fussy eater

Most young children have good days and bad days when it comes to eating, but if your child is going through a fussy eating stage that lasts longer than a few weeks, it's easy to find yourself getting stressed out. Don't despair – help is at hand!

I t's thought that fussy eating stems from an inherent, evolutionary trait that is designed to protect us from ingesting anything harmful. Known as food neophobia, this natural emotion seems to kick in just when your toddler is learning to assert himself, which can cause him – and you – a good deal of misery! Try these ideas to restore meal-time harmony:

1 Doctor, doctor. If fussy eating lasts longer than a few weeks, see your GP to rule out any health problems. Teething or an infection are enough to put anyone off their food.

2 Don't get stressed! A child refusing to eat can lead to tears all round – be patient and keep calm. If you've tried and failed to get your little one interested in his dinner, take it away and move onto something else. Remember, if he sees his behaviour gets a reaction, then he's likely to try this again to get more attention.

3 Small but perfectly formed. Toddlers can find large portions overwhelming, so try him with smaller portions until he regains his appetite.

4 Peer pressure. Invite other toddlers with healthy appetites over for tea or eat with your children. Toddlers learn by copying others so if he sees other children or the rest of the family tucking in, it will encourage him to eat better.

5 Vary your approach. If your toddler refuses to eat home-made purées or jarred foods, try him with finger foods instead. Toddlers often look to take charge of their eating, so finger foods may give him the control he's seeking.

6 Location, location, location. Is your child more co-operative when you're out and about or at someone else's home? Perhaps varying where he eats will help with his feeding issues.

7 Praise him, praise him! There's nothing like words of encouragement and praise to get your little one back on the eating track.

8 Think outside the box. Try seeing things from his point of view. Maybe he'd rather feed himself, or perhaps he doesn't like the texture of his food, or the way it's been cut up. Just by offering food in a different way, you can re-boot your toddler's feeding.

9 Presentation is everything! Well, not quite, but food that looks interesting and appealing is more likely to attract their attention.

10 Try, try again! Don't stress at his refusal. Try the same food at another meal and keep on trying it.

11 Limit snacks. If your little one is struggling at meal-times, make sure he's actually hungry. If he's filled up on drinks or snacks earlier in the day, he's unlikely to show much interest in his tea.

12 Routine. Toddlers like a set routine, so stick to what they know. Regular meal times mean he will know what to expect – and when.

13 Meet them half way! If your older toddler is going through a phase where only junk food will do, then make your own, but healthier! And use that old standby of hiding the veg he doesn't like among the tasty foods he does like.

14 Get them involved. Toddlers are naturally inquisitive, so get them involved in preparing their food or at least let them watch you making it.

15 Sound effects. Toddlers are easily distracted by noise, toys or games – particularly when food is on the table, so try to aim for a calm atmosphere at meal times.

Mini pork meatballs

Toddlers will love these little meatballs that are just right for eating with a spoon. Fussy eaters won't notice the veg in the meatballs and sauce

1 medium courgette

450g lean pork mince

2 spring onions, trimmed and roughly chopped

1 large egg yolk

1 tbsp vegetable oil

1 medium carrot, coarsely grated

½ tsp dried thyme

400g tin Sainsbury's Basics chopped tomatoes in tomato juice

1 tbsp tomato purée

Cooked macaroni and grated Parmesan, to serve

1 Coarsely grate the courgette into a large bowl. Pat dry with kitchen paper to remove as much of the excess liquid as possible. Add the pork mince, half the spring onions and the egg yolk. Combine well, then using your hands, shape the mixture into 24 little balls.

2 Heat the oil in a large, deep-sided frying pan (preferably non-stick). Cook the meatballs in batches for 5-8 mins or until golden all over.

3 Transfer the meatballs to a plate, and set aside. Add the remaining spring onions to the pan along with the carrot and thyme. Cook for 5 mins, stirring occasionally, until the onions have softened a bit. Stir in the tomatoes.

4 Pour 150ml boiling water into a measuring jug and stir in the tomato purée, then pour into the pan. Return the meatballs to the pan, bring to the boil, cover and reduce the heat to a simmer for 15 mins, adding a little more water if necessary.

5 Serve the meatballs with cooked macaroni and a sprinkling of Parmesan, if you like.

 Suitable for freezing (see p7 for information)

 **Owen says:** *'These were so quick to make and my children made them disappear just as quickly! Angelo had six and Ella ate three. They were really tasty and easy – 10 out of 10!'*

Slow-cooked beef stew

This one pot, big batch recipe makes enough to serve 8 toddlers
but it's easy to freeze any leftovers

2 tbsp vegetable or
olive oil
1 medium onion, sliced
1 garlic clove,
slightly squashed
1 tbsp plain flour
400g pack Sainsbury's
SO organic diced beef,
or 485g pack Sainsbury's
lean diced casserole steak
700ml low-salt beef stock
(such as Kallo)
1 tsp tomato purée
1 tsp English mustard
1 tsp balsamic vinegar
2 medium carrots,
roughly chopped
2 large parsnips (or
3 medium ones), peeled
and roughly chopped

1 Preheat the oven to 150°C, fan 130°C, gas 2.
2 Heat half the oil in a heavy-based pan and gently
sauté the onion and garlic until soft and pale golden –
this will take at least 10 mins – then transfer the
mixture to a large casserole.
3 Sprinkle the flour onto a large plate, add the diced
beef and turn to coat in the flour. Heat the remaining
oil in the pan until really hot and fry the beef pieces in
batches so that it becomes nicely brown, then add
them to the casserole.
4 Tip any remaining flour into the frying pan, then add
the stock, tomato purée, mustard, and vinegar. Scrape
the bottom of the pan with a wooden spoon to loosen
any bits that are stuck.
5 Pour into the casserole, add the carrots and parsnips,
cover with a lid and cook for 3 hours in the oven or until
the meat is tender. You will need to check the stew
during cooking and add more water if it needs it. Serve
with steamed broccoli florets, if you like.

 Suitable for freezing (see p7 for information)

Grilled plaice with parsley sauce

If you like, add a handful of frozen peas to the sauce and cook for a few minutes. Adding parsley to the sauce is a way of introducing your toddler to new and interesting flavours

1 tbsp unsalted butter, plus extra for grilling
1 tbsp plain flour
300ml Sainsbury's whole milk
A few stalks of fresh parsley
2 Sainsbury's fresh plaice fillets
Juice of ¼ lemon

1 Put the butter, flour and milk into a small saucepan and whisk over a low heat until you have a smooth sauce – about 5-8 mins.
2 Cut the stalks off the parsley, then finely chop the leaves and add to the sauce.
3 Heat the grill to high. Dot the fish with a little butter and drizzle with the lemon juice, then grill for 5-8 mins or until the fish is cooked through.
4 Remove the skin from the fish and flake half a fillet into a bowl – checking very carefully for bones – then drizzle over some sauce. Serve with mashed potato and some steamed veg.

 Suitable for freezing (see p7 for information)

Tropical fruit sundae

Tropical fruit sundae

SERVES 2 ADULTS + 2 TODDLERS. PREP TIME: 5 MINS.

Spoon Sainsbury's tropical crunchy oat cereal into four glasses – allow about 3 tbsp for the adults and 2 tbsp for the children (check there are no big lumps). Add a similar quantity of Sainsbury's Greek yogurt to each glass and finish with a top layer of your favourite tropical fruits. Chop the fruits to the appropriate size for your toddlers.

Pea and ham risotto

Spoons are the simplest piece of cutlery for toddlers to master, and this sticky risotto can be easily scooped from bowl to mouth

1 tbsp olive oil
½ onion, finely chopped
100g Sainsbury's
basmati rice
150g Sainsbury's frozen
garden peas
50g ham, finely sliced
2 tbsp crème fraîche

1 Heat the oil in a deep frying pan until hot. Add the onion and sauté until just tender.
2 Add the rice to the pan and stir to combine with the onion.
3 Pour in 450ml boiling water and simmer for 10-12 mins or until the rice is tender. Stir in the peas and ham. Cook for a few mins until they are heated through and the liquid has reduced.
4 Stir in the crème fraîche before serving.

 Suitable for freezing (see p7 for information)

SERVES 4 TODDLERS
PREP TIME: 5 MINS
COOK TIME: 2 HOURS

Lemon and raisin rice pudding

This is best eaten the day that it is made or kept in the fridge for up to a couple of days and eaten cold

Butter, for greasing

70g pudding rice

600ml milk

1 capful Sainsbury's Taste the Difference Madagascan vanilla extract

Zest of 1 lemon or 1 orange

1 ½ tbsp golden caster sugar

3 tbsp raisins

1 Preheat the oven to 150ºC, fan 130ºC, gas 2. Butter an ovenproof dish.
2 Stir all the ingredients together in the dish and bake for 2 hours in the oven. Stir 2 or 3 times during cooking for extra creaminess.
3 Allow to cool before serving.

SERVES 4 TODDLERS
PREP TIME: 15-20 MINS
COOK TIME: 20-25 MINS

Salmon filo pies

Salmon is an oily fish, so it contains omega-3, which is important for the healthy development of your toddler's brain and eyesight

A little butter (about 5g), plus extra melted butter for brushing

2 tsp olive oil

4 spring onions or baby leeks, trimmed and finely chopped

6 tbsp Sainsbury's half-fat crème fraîche or mascarpone

Squeeze of lemon juice

Small handful fresh finely chopped dill or parsley

2 Sainsbury's salmon fillets (each about 125g), cut into pieces

8 sheets filo pastry

1 Preheat the oven to 180°C, fan 160°C, gas 4. Heat the butter and oil in a small pan and sauté the spring onions or leeks for about 5 mins or until soft.

2 Add the crème fraîche or mascarpone, lemon juice and herbs, and mix together. Remove from the heat, then add the salmon and stir gently.

3 Brush melted butter onto 2 sheets of filo pastry and put one on top of the other. Repeat with the remaining sheets so that you have 4 portions, each made from 2 sheets of pastry.

4 Divide the salmon mixture between the pastry sheets and wrap the pastry around the filling to make 4 parcels.

5 Put the parcels onto a non-stick baking tray and bake in the oven for 15 mins or until the salmon is cooked and the pastry is golden and crisp. Serve with vegetables of your choice or salad.

Ham, pea and cheese macaroni bake

A great dish for toddlers to tuck into with a knife and fork. The cheese and milk provide calcium to help build healthy bones

100g Sainsbury's macaroni

50g frozen peas

15g unsalted butter

1 tbsp plain flour

200ml Sainsbury's whole milk

50g ham, roughly chopped

50g Sainsbury's British mild Cheddar, grated

50g fresh breadcrumbs

1 Preheat the oven to 200°C, fan 180°C, gas 6. Add the macaroni to a pan of boiling water and cook for 10-12 mins; add the peas for the final 2 mins of the cooking time.

2 Meanwhile, melt the butter in a pan and stir in the flour with a wooden spoon. Slowly add the milk, stirring continuously. Bring to the boil and cook for 2 mins, then stir in the ham and Cheddar.

3 Drain the macaroni and peas, then stir through the cheese sauce. Pour into a small baking dish and top with the breadcrumbs.

4 Bake in the hot oven for 10-15 mins, until the top is golden and bubbling.

Mild Thai fish curry

Serve this with rice, noodles or bread – starchy foods should make up around half of each meal at this stage of your toddler's development

1 tbsp vegetable oil

2 spring onions, trimmed and chopped

1 yellow pepper, deseeded and cut into small pieces

2 tsp Sainsbury's Thai green curry paste

400ml tin reduced fat coconut milk

Juice of 1 lime

1 tsp light soft brown sugar

100g sugar snap peas

2 Sainsbury's skinless and boneless fresh haddock fillets (check for any bones)

Handful fresh chopped coriander

1 Heat the oil in a saucepan, add the spring onions and yellow pepper and sauté gently until slightly soft – about 3-4 mins.

2 Add the curry paste and cook for 1 min.

3 Add the coconut milk, lime juice and sugar and taste – if it's too spicy, add a little more coconut milk.

4 Cut the sugar snap peas into thirds, add them to the pan and cook for 2 mins.

5 Add the haddock and coriander and cook for another 3-4 mins or until the fish is cooked through. Serve with rice, noodles or bread.

SERVES 4 TODDLERS
PREP TIME: 10-15 MINS
COOK TIME: 30 MINS

Stuffed courgettes  Ⓥ

The raisins in this dish add a hint of sweetness, contain iron, and provide potassium

2 medium courgettes

1 tbsp olive oil

1 small garlic clove, finely chopped

1 carrot, grated

4 tbsp cooked couscous

2 tbsp raisins

1 tbsp finely shredded fresh basil leaves

1 free-range egg, lightly beaten

30g Sainsbury's British mild Cheddar, grated

1 Preheat the oven to 200°C, fan 180°C, gas 6. Cook the courgettes whole in a large pan of boiling water for 5 mins. Drain, then leave to cool slightly. Halve lengthways and scoop out the flesh. Set aside the hollowed-out halves and roughly chop the cooked flesh.

2 Heat the oil in a frying pan, add the chopped courgette flesh and garlic, and cook for about 5 mins over a medium heat, until golden. Transfer to a large bowl and mix in the grated carrot, couscous, raisins, basil, beaten egg and most of the grated Cheddar.

3 Spoon the mixture back into the courgette halves and scatter the reserved grated Cheddar over the top.

4 Arrange the courgettes in a large baking dish and bake for 20 mins, until the egg is set and the tops are golden brown.

SERVES 4 TODDLERS
PREP TIME: 15 MINS
COOK TIME: 25-30 MINS

Mild vegetable chilli with kidney beans (v)

Start with small amounts of cumin and chilli and adjust to taste. Giving your toddler new flavours to try means they're less likely to be fussy eaters later on

1 tbsp olive oil

1 onion, finely chopped

1 courgette, trimmed and chopped into fine dice

4 Sainsbury's mushrooms, chopped

1 red pepper, deseeded and cut into small pieces

½-1 tsp mild chilli powder

½-1 tsp cumin powder

400g chopped tomatoes

2 tbsp tomato purée

215g tin Sainsbury's red kidney beans in water, drained and rinsed

1 Heat the oil in a heavy-based saucepan, add the onion, courgette, mushrooms and pepper and cook gently for about 10 mins or until soft.

2 Add the chilli and cumin and cook for a few mins.

3 Add the chopped tomatoes, tomato purée and kidney beans and gently simmer for 15 mins.

4 Serve wrapped in a tortilla or with couscous.

 Suitable for freezing (see p7 for information)

Sage and breadcrumb chicken escalopes

A great meal for toddlers to perfect their knife and fork skills — and they'll love the crumb coating on the chicken

2 Sainsbury's free-range
chicken breast fillets
2 tbsp plain flour
1 free-range egg
4 fresh sage leaves,
finely chopped
6 tbsp fresh breadcrumbs
2 tbsp olive oil

1 Put the chicken breasts in between 2 pieces of clingfilm and bash with a rolling pin until flattened.
2 Put the flour into a bowl, then crack the egg into a separate bowl and beat lightly. Put the chopped sage and breadcrumbs into a third bowl.
3 Dip the flattened chicken into the flour, then in the egg, and finally in the breadcrumb mixture, turning to coat well.
4 Heat the oil in a heavy-based frying pan over a medium heat and cook for about 6-7 mins on one side until golden, then turn over and fry for another 3-4 mins on the other side until golden and the chicken is cooked through. Cut into strips and serve half a chicken breast to each toddler with boiled new potatoes, peas and ketchup or salad and bread.

Tip...
You could also
try making this
dish with pork
escalopes or
turkey fillets.

Very veggie couscous (v)

If you're pressed for time, this is a tasty, super quick dish you can put together quickly with storecupboard staples and veg from the fridge

150g couscous
1 spring onion, trimmed
and finely chopped
1 carrot, grated
¼ cucumber,
finely chopped
2 cherry tomatoes,
finely chopped
Large handful raisins
1 tsp lemon juice or
white wine vinegar
2 tbsp olive oil

1 Put the couscous into a bowl, cover with 175ml boiling water, then cover the bowl with clingfilm and leave until the grains have absorbed the water. Fluff up with a fork.
2 Add the spring onion, carrot, cucumber, tomatoes and raisins, and mix together.
3 Mix together the lemon juice or vinegar and oil, pour over the couscous, mix and serve.

‘ *Give your little ones some sticks of veg to munch on while you rustle up this dish* ’

ANNIE DENNY, SAINSBURY'S NUTRITIONIST

' It's great when one dish fits the bill for everyone so Wev can't wait until Rohan's able to eat with us too!

Sanjay and Sarah Singh, Dad and Mum to Layla, 22 months, and Rohan, 20 weeks

Family eating

Something for everyone

M eals that appeal to every member of the family are worth their weight in gold. After all, if you can feed everyone with just one dish, you'll save time, hassle and money, not to mention loads of washing up!

Children learn eating habits from you, so regularly eating together as a family is the best way to encourage a healthy, balanced attitude to food. It's a great way to tackle fussy eating, too. Working hours sometimes rule out family meals during the week so, if you can, make weekend meals special family occasions when everyone sits down together, takes time over a meal and talks.

Adapting meals for family eating

With just a few simple adaptations, you can make family favourites suitable and appealing for babies, toddlers, older children and grown-ups, too. All our recipes on the following pages have been adapted for your little ones, with ingredients the whole family will enjoy, so you can build up a repertoire of meals they'll ask for time and time again.

One of the main changes you should make is to reduce the amount of sugar you use and avoid salt. It's best not to add these during the cooking process – wait until the dish is cooked, reserve a portion for your baby and toddler, then add seasoning to suit the rest of the family. Use low-salt stock or water when cooking, and remember that many pre-prepared sauces and condiments can be high in both salt and sugar.

Do include whole milk in recipes. As well as providing calcium, whole milk helps ensure that weaning babies and toddlers get sufficient calories for their needs.

Boosting fruit and veg

Eating as a family also gives you a chance to boost your little one's intake of fruits and

Easy ways to get them to five or more a day

- Throw a couple of handfuls of frozen mixed vegetables into the pan of simmering water when you're cooking pasta, then drain and mix with tinned tomatoes.

- Make soup! Use whatever you have in the veg drawer, add fun pasta shapes and serve with grated Parmesan for the adults.

- Add diced apple to tomato-based sauces to balance acidity and give a hint of natural sweetness.

- Experiment with mashed potato by adding parsnips, sweet potato and carrots. These make great toppings for fish or cottage pie.

- Add chopped fresh fruit to cereal or porridge.

- Make desserts based on fruit. Serve baked apples or bananas, or fun fruit kebabs with a dollop of plain yogurt.

- Add dried fruit such as raisins or apricots to home-made flapjacks (see the recipe on p158).

MY STORY

'The hardest part of family cooking is knowing what to make. We're always looking for inspiration, so having a good store of recipes is essential.'

Sanjay Singh, Dad to Layla, 22 months, and Rohan, 20 weeks

vegetables. Not every child hates fruit and veg – many will happily munch their way through a bowl of fruit or a plate of carrot sticks. But if it isn't on her list of 'favourite foods', there are lots of ways to make sure she still gets her five-a-day. Whether it's blending vegetables into a pasta sauce or whizzing fruit into a smoothie, often all it takes is a little creative thinking and they'll be coming back for more! See the panel, left, for other ideas.

Smart servings

Help keep toddlers enthusiastic about mealtimes by giving them their own colourful plates, bowls, cutlery and placemats. For younger babies and toddlers, you will need to purée, mash or cut up food so that it's a manageable consistency or size. Always ensure that the food is cool enough for them to eat without burning their mouth, and always double check fish dishes for any small bones. Finally, don't serve portions to toddlers that are too big as they can be daunted by too much food on their plate (see p92 for more on this) – you can always give them seconds if they want more.

EAT WITH THE FAMILY!

Eating together as a family has lots of benefits. Interaction at the table helps develop a child's social skills and promotes happier family relationships. Plus, research suggests that the more often children eat meals with family members, the healthier their diet is likely to be later in life.

Eating together as a family can also help when it comes to toddlers who are fussy eaters (for more on this, see p95). Toddlers who see their mum, dad and siblings enjoying different foods will be encouraged to try new things for themselves. And the more flavours a child is exposed to, the less likely it is that they will be fussy about food.

TIPS FOR HAPPY FAMILY MEALTIMES

Avoid distractions, such as television. Make a point of announcing that it is dinner time and treat it as an important part of the day.

Make mealtimes fun with plenty of conversation and praise.

Try to establish a routine by having meals at the same time each day. This gives your child a sense of stability and security.

Be realistic about how long your toddler will sit still at the table. Younger children may get restless quickly. Put a time limit on how long they should stay at the table.

Let your child have some choice in what they're eating by allowing them to select, say, two out of three different vegetables on offer.

Try to avoid negative remarks about food – if you show you don't like something, this will be noticed by your toddler. Make plenty of encouraging noises and comment positively on food. Don't offer bribes of foods they like to get them to eat food they're not keen on.

Let your little one eat at their own pace and don't insist they finish everything on their plate. Mealtimes should be enjoyable – if it's stressful, they could lose their appetite and become even fussier.

Money-saving tips

The takeaways, ready-meals and deli ingredients you loved as a couple can become too expensive when your family starts to grow. Here are some tips from savvy mums on how to make your budget work:

Cook from scratch

Meals made from scratch are often more cost-effective and healthier than ready-meals or takeaways and they needn't be complicated. The family-friendly meals you'll find in the following pages are all easy to make, even if you're a kitchen novice!

Don't waste food

If you have food leftover after a meal, don't throw it away. It will usually keep for up to two days in the fridge (however leftover seafood is best eaten within one day). Store leftovers in a sealed container or in a dish covered with clingfilm, away from raw meat. They can be used as the basis for a new dish the following day. Also, they're more satisfying than a sandwich for lunch! Pack cold leftovers in a plastic storage box inside a cool bag with an ice pack for school lunches.

Eat seasonally

Fruits, vegetables and even some fish and shellfish are cheaper when in season as you're more likely to see special offers at these times.

Make more with eggs

With six eggs, some onions and potato, you've got the basis of a Spanish omelette that can feed a family of four. Just add a side serving of frozen peas or green beans.

Bake your own bread

If you have a breadmaker, dust it off and start using it! Home-made is often cheaper and there's nothing like coming down to the smell of baking bread in the morning.

Switch and save

Swap branded products for Sainsbury's own brand or Basics ranges when it comes to foods you use a lot of, such as breakfast cereals, porridge, potatoes, rice and pasta.

Try something new

Try using cheaper cuts of meat, such as beef skirt, neck of lamb or chicken thighs, which are great in stews and casseroles. Also try less common fish, such as coley and pollock, which are often cheaper than the popular cod, haddock and salmon.

Plan it out

Planning meals for the week helps you keep your budget on track. For example, if you want to cook something special one night, make an inexpensive pasta dish the next, to balance the cost.

Use your freezer

Buying larger size packs or cooking in bulk and freezing can save money and time. Try the recipe for roasted vegetable pasta sauce on p140 - it makes two family portions of sauce so you chill or freeze one for another day.

Look out for special offers

Coupons, vouchers and offers can save you money - look out for those on the Little Ones website - www.sainsburys.co.uk/littleones - and in the Little Ones magazines. Use your Nectar card and tot up your points online. You can use them at a range of top-name stores, as well as Sainsbury's.

MY STORY

'I was determined to cook everything myself and I'm proud of the fact the girls have never had a ready-meal for dinner. My secret is to cook in big batches and freeze it for when we're busy. That way, I always know what's in it and it saves me spending hours in the kitchen. I just leave it to defrost and add fresh veg.'

**Jenny Breadmore,
Mum to Daisy, 3, Ruby, 12 months**

Planning and shopping

Making family meals that are tasty, varied and nutritious for everyone – as well as cost effective – is all about planning ahead, using your time wisely, and getting the whole family involved

1 Make a list
Planning meals means you can make a shopping list of all the things you'll need. Having a shopping list – and sticking to it – saves you time and money at the supermarket.

2 Shop online
Explore the option of shopping for your groceries online. It's a great time saver and you can find all the current offers on one page. Visit www.sainsburys.co.uk to learn more.

3 Time it right
Have a few quick recipe ideas up your sleeve using storecupboard ingredients (see right). Use these when time is tight, and save trickier recipes for more relaxed days.

4 Make extra
Set aside time for cooking at the weekend to stock the fridge and freezer for the week ahead. Double-up on portions and there'll be something in the freezer for when there's no time to cook from scratch.

5 Make sure meals are nutritionally balanced
For many people this is second nature, but it's worth pausing from time to time and asking yourself whether meals are as healthy as they could be. If in doubt, add more fruit and veg!

6 Share the workload
Planning, shopping and cooking family meals is a big job, so ask other family members to lend a hand to take the pressure off.

7 Try new ideas
We all love traditional family favourites, but trying some new recipes helps keep everyone enthusiastic about mealtimes. Ask friends and family for ideas, and start a file of your favourites.

8 Grow your own
Growing fresh herbs is easy, even if you don't have much space, and you can use them in just about everything to add flavour and variety to your cooking.

9 Add some variety
Putting a twist on regular standbys will keep things interesting. Adding just one unusual ingredient can make an everyday dish special. Try our roast pork with prune and sage stuffing on p142.

10 Keep a well-stocked storecupboard
A well-stocked storecupboard with plenty of staples will save you money, as you can buy in bulk. It also allows you to prepare simple, last-minute meals.

Store cupboard essentials:

Rice: Forms the basis of many dishes including risotto, kedgeree and biryanis.

Tinned fish: Choose varieties in water or oil rather than brine. Great for pasta bakes and home-made fish cakes. Mash with cooked potato, shape into patties, dip in beaten egg, then breadcrumbs and shallow fry in rapeseed oil.

Pasta: Easy to jazz up with a ready-made sauce, along with some sautéed broccoli, cherry tomatoes and pieces of chicken.

Couscous: It's quick, easy and cheap – see our recipe on p112.

Low-salt stock: Adds flavour to curries, stews and soups. Choose a low-salt stock when cooking for little ones, such as Sainsbury's Signature stocks.

Dried herbs: They add essential flavour to your food when you don't have any fresh herbs on hand.

Tinned tomatoes: Use as a base for pasta sauce or a vegetable soup, then freeze in batches. For a simple meal, simmer a tin of tomatoes with 1 litre low-salt stock and 100g red lentils for 20 mins, and serve with grilled pitta bread.

Baked beans: The ultimate standby, use as a filling for a baked potato or simply serve on toast. Look for the reduced-sugar and reduced-salt version for babies and toddlers.

Tinned fruit: Kids love tinned fruit, and it's a good standby for dessert. Look for fruit in juice rather than sugary syrup.

Roasted sausages with vegetables

Serve two sausages to the adults and one to each of the toddlers.
Purée just the veg for the baby and try serving it with crushed
hard-boiled egg for added protein

1 red pepper and 1 orange
pepper, deseeded and cut
into chunks
1 red onion, cut into
thin wedges
1 courgette, trimmed and
cut into chunks
500g bag Sainsbury's mini
new potatoes, halved
2 garlic cloves (skin on)
454g pack Sainsbury's
Be good to yourself
Cumberland sausages
2 tbsp olive oil
1 sprig fresh rosemary
(optional)

1 Preheat the oven to 180°C, fan 160°C, gas 4.
2 Put the peppers, onion, courgette, potatoes
and garlic into a roasting tin, then lay the
sausages on top.
3 Drizzle over the oil and tuck the rosemary in
between the vegetables, if using. Roast for 30
mins. Turn the sausages over and roast for
another 15-20 mins or until the potatoes are
tender and the sausages are cooked and golden.
**For toddlers, allow to cool before cutting up the
sausages and serving with the veg.**

Sarah says: *'With all the ingredients cooking in one roasting tin, this
was really easy to make. It looked very appealing on the plate and my
husband, Layla and I really enjoyed eating it!'*

Sweetcorn and fish chowder with cornbread

A classic soup that will warm the cockles on a chilly evening. The cornbread makes a delicious change from ordinary bread

20g unsalted butter

2 shallots, finely chopped

1 garlic clove, chopped

300g butternut squash, cubed

2 medium floury potatoes, cubed

300ml Sainsbury's Signature vegetable stock

100ml Sainsbury's double cream

300ml Sainsbury's whole milk

300g frozen sweetcorn

300g cod loin, cubed

Small bunch flat-leaf parsley, chopped

FOR THE CORNBREAD

125g polenta

125g plain flour

2 tsp baking powder

½ tsp bicarbonate of soda

1 bunch spring onions, finely chopped

50g mature Cheddar, grated

2 medium free-range eggs

150g natural yogurt

150ml Sainsbury's whole milk

25g unsalted butter, melted

1 Preheat the oven to 200°C, fan 180°C, gas 6. Grease and line a 23cm square baking tin.

2 Make the cornbread. In a large bowl, mix together the polenta, flour, baking powder, bicarbonate of soda, spring onions and Cheddar. Make a well in the centre of the dry ingredients and set aside.

3 In a separate bowl, whisk together the eggs, yogurt, milk and butter. Pour this mixture into the dry ingredients and stir until everything is combined. Pour the batter into the lined tin and bake for 20 mins until golden.

4 Meanwhile, make the chowder. Melt the butter in a large saucepan and gently cook the shallots and garlic for 3 mins until softened. Stir in the squash and potatoes, and cook for a further 5 mins. Pour over the vegetable stock, double cream and milk, and bring to a gentle simmer.

5 Add the sweetcorn and simmer for 5 mins. Using either a hand-held blender or a free-standing blender, purée half of the mixture until smooth. Return the puréed mixture to the pan, add the fish (check for any small bones first) and parsley, and cook for a further 5 mins until the fish is opaque. Serve the chowder and cornbread together.

For toddlers, serve when cooled.

SERVES 2 ADULTS, 2
TODDLERS + 1 BABY
PREP TIME: 10-15 MINS
COOK TIME: 25 MINS

Cauliflower, macaroni and tomato gratin ⓥ

A really tasty and satisfying macaroni cheese with extra goodness added, in the form of cauliflower, spring onions and tomatoes

250g dried macaroni

300g cauliflower, broken into florets

50g unsalted butter

50g plain flour

600ml Sainsbury's whole milk

100g mature Cheddar, grated

1 tsp Dijon mustard

½ x 25g pack Sainsbury's fresh chives, snipped

Bunch spring onions, trimmed and finely sliced

200g Sainsbury's cherry tomatoes, halved

25g fresh breadcrumbs

1 Bring a large pan of water to the boil and cook the macaroni for 5 mins, then add the cauliflower florets and cook for a further 3 mins, or until the pasta is cooked. Drain well and return to the pan.

2 Melt the butter in a medium saucepan and add the flour. Beat together until you have a smooth paste. Remove from the hob and gradually pour in the milk, stirring continuously with a wooden spoon until smooth. Return to the heat and bring to a simmer, stirring until the mixture is thick enough to coat the back of the spoon.

3 Stir in three-quarters of the grated Cheddar, along with the mustard and chives until well combined. Pour the cheesy sauce over the cooked macaroni and cauliflower, add the spring onions and mix well.

4 Preheat the grill to high. Spoon the macaroni mixture into a 2-litre ovenproof dish and scatter the cherry tomato halves over the top. Sprinkle over the breadcrumbs and remaining Cheddar and place under the hot grill for about 5 mins, until it is crisp and golden on top.

For toddlers, serve the cheesy macaroni with steamed broccoli florets or their favourite green veg. For baby, purée to the right consistency.

Vegetable curry ⓥ

The coconut milk, butternut squash and peppers give this dish
a creamy texture and sweetness that little ones will love. If you
like, add cooked chicken or prawns to the curry

1 tbsp vegetable oil
1 large onion, sliced
2 tbsp tikka masala paste
200ml reduced-fat
coconut milk
200ml very low-salt
vegetable stock,
such as Kallo
½ butternut squash
(about 250g), deseeded
and cubed
250g Sainsbury's
green beans, trimmed
and cut in half
1 red pepper, deseeded
and chopped
Fresh coriander leaves,
to garnish

1 Heat the oil in a large pan and fry the onion
over a medium heat for 5 mins until softened. Stir
in the masala paste and cook for 1 min. Turn down
the heat and pour in the coconut milk, stirring well.
2 Slowly pour in the stock. Add the butternut
squash and bring to the boil, then lower the heat,
cover and simmer for about 10 mins.
3 Add the beans and chopped pepper to the pan
and cook, covered, for another 5-10 mins until the
squash is tender. Garnish with coriander and serve
with pilau rice and naan bread or chapattis.
**For toddlers, serve when cooled to the right
temperature - you may need to cut the
vegetables smaller for your little one.**

Tip...
For baby, purée the broth with the chicken, carrots, celery, onion and a few noodles (before step 3). Add more broth to get the right consistency.

Spring chicken noodle soup

This soup can be messy for toddlers to eat but great fun!
Substitute their favourite vegetables for any they don't like here

2 tbsp olive oil

1 onion, finely chopped

2 carrots, finely diced

2 celery sticks, trimmed
and finely chopped

2 garlic cloves,
finely chopped

1 tbsp fresh ginger, grated

1.5 litres Sainsbury's
Signature vegetable
stock, hot

4 Sainsbury's free-range
skinless chicken thigh
fillets, cut into small pieces

200g medium egg noodles

1 bunch Sainsbury's
spring onions, trimmed
and finely chopped

100g sugar snap peas,
halved lengthways

100g green
cabbage, shredded

1 tbsp reduced-salt soy
sauce (optional)

1 Heat the olive oil in a large saucepan, add the onion, carrots and celery, and cook for about 8-10 mins until beginning to soften but not colour. Add the garlic and ginger, and cook for a few more mins. Pour over the hot stock and simmer for 10 mins, then add the chicken and cook for a further 10 mins.

2 Meanwhile, bring a medium saucepan of water to the boil, add the noodles and cook for 3 mins until tender. Drain well and refresh under cold running water.

3 Add the spring onions, sugar snap peas and cabbage to the vegetable and chicken broth, and simmer for 5 mins.

4 Divide the noodles between bowls and ladle the broth over the top. Flavour with the low-salt soy sauce, if using.

For toddlers, make sure the soup is cool enough for them before serving. Give them a spoon to slurp the broth with and a fork to scoop up the noodles.

Easy lasagne

A great family favourite – the chopped onion, red pepper
and celery add texture, flavour and extra vitamins

1 tbsp olive or vegetable oil
1 onion, finely chopped
1 red pepper, deseeded
and finely chopped
1 celery stick,
finely chopped
400g Sainsbury's
SO organic British beef
lean steak mince,
or Sainsbury's lean
steak mince
400g tin chopped
tomatoes
2 tbsp tomato purée
Pinch of brown sugar
About 12 Sainsbury's
lasagne pasta sheets
400g jar Sainsbury's
white sauce with cheese
20g Parmesan
cheese, grated

1 Preheat the oven to 180°C, fan 160°C, gas 4. Heat
the oil in a heavy-based pan, add the onion, pepper
and celery, and sauté gently for at least 10 mins until
really soft. Add the mince and cook until slightly
browned. Add the chopped tomatoes and half a tin
(200ml) of water, the tomato purée and sugar.
Simmer gently for 20 mins, stirring often.
2 Spoon a little of the mince mixture into the bottom
of 2 ovenproof dishes. Top with enough pasta sheets
to cover - you might need to break the sheets in half
to fit in your dish.
3 Top with another layer of mince and then
a third of the jar of white sauce. Cover with a second
layer of pasta sheets. Spoon the rest of the mince
over the top and another third of the jar of sauce -
just dot the sauce over, it doesn't need to be a thick
layer as it will spread in the oven when it cooks.
4 Top with a final layer of pasta sheets and the
remaining white sauce. Sprinkle over the cheese and
bake for 30-35 mins until the pasta is cooked and
the top is golden.
**Cut up for your toddler and mash or purée
for baby.**

 Suitable for freezing (see p7 for information)

MAKES 2 QUICHES, EACH
SERVES 2 ADULTS
+ 2 TODDLERS
PREP TIME: 20 MINS
COOK TIME: 35 MINS

Ham, cheese and herb quiches

This makes two meals and the second quiche will keep in the fridge for up to two days – perfect for picnics or packed lunches

375g shortcrust pastry

6 Sainsbury's free-range eggs

150ml double cream

150ml semi-skimmed milk

Large handful fresh chopped flat-leaf parsley

40g mature Cheddar, grated

1 pack Taste the Difference honey roast Wiltshire ham (4 slices), chopped

1 Preheat the oven to 180°C, fan 160°C, gas 4. Roll the pastry out to fit 2 x 20cm flan tins, then line the tins with the pastry. Trim the edges and prick the bases with a fork. Line with greaseproof paper and fill with baking beans, rice or pasta, then blind bake for 10 mins. Remove the beans and greaseproof paper and bake for another 5 mins.

2 Crack the eggs into a bowl, add the cream, milk and chopped parsley and whisk with a fork. Scatter the cheese and ham over the tarts, then divide the egg mixture between them.

3 Bake for 20 mins or until cooked through. Serve with salad.

For toddlers, allow to cool then cut up and serve with lettuce and tomatoes.

SERVES 2 ADULTS +
2 TODDLERS
PREP TIME: 15 MINS
COOK TIME: 25-30 MINS

Tuna fishcakes

Simple and delicious – these are great partners for fresh steamed veg.
Leek, lemon zest and fresh chives give them a real flavour boost

700g floury potatoes, such
as King Edward or Maris
Piper, cubed
3 tbsp olive oil
1 large leek (about 150g),
trimmed, halved
lengthways and
finely chopped
200g tin Sainsbury's
Albacore tuna steaks in
spring water, drained
Finely grated zest
of 1 lemon
3 tbsp chopped
fresh chives
50g Sainsbury's mild
Cheddar, grated
2 tbsp plain flour

1 Put the potatoes in a large saucepan and cover with cold water. Bring to the boil and cook for 8-10 mins until tender. Drain, then return to the pan and mash until smooth.

2 Meanwhile, heat 1 tbsp of the oil in a frying pan, add the leek and cook for 5 mins until tender. Remove from the heat and place in a large bowl.

3 Add the tuna to the leeks along with the mashed potatoes, lemon zest, chives and cheese. Mix well and let it cool slightly.

4 Shape into 8 round cakes. Sprinkle the flour onto a plate and use it to dust each fishcake.

5 Heat the remaining oil in a large frying pan and cook the fishcakes over a low heat for 3-4 mins each side until golden and crunchy on the outside and heated through. You may need to cook them in batches so the pan is not overcrowded.

Serve 1 fishcake with steamed green beans for each toddler or, if you like, you could serve them cold with a fresh salad.

❄ **Suitable for freezing (see p7 for information)**

Chicken with a creamy sauce

This is an easy, one-pan family supper dish – and you'll find that toddlers will just love the creamy, slightly piquant sauce

Small piece of butter

1 tbsp olive oil

6 Sainsbury's Taste the Difference chicken thigh fillets or 3 Sainsbury's chicken breasts

1 shallot, finely chopped

1 garlic clove, crushed

200ml low-salt chicken stock, such as Kallo or Sainsbury's Signature

150ml Sainsbury's single cream

1 tbsp wholegrain mustard

A small handful (about 10) fresh tarragon leaves, chopped

1 Heat the butter and oil in a frying pan and sauté the chicken thighs or breasts for a few mins on each side until golden brown.

2 Push the chicken to one side of the pan, add the shallot and garlic and cook gently until soft.

3 Add the stock, cream and mustard and simmer very gently until the sauce has reduced and the chicken is cooked – this will take about 10 mins.

4 Add the chopped tarragon and leave to simmer for a few mins. Add freshly ground black pepper to taste. Serve with green beans and rice or salad and new potatoes.

For toddlers, cool to the right temperature and whizz or cut up the chicken pieces to a manageable size for your little one.

' Chicken is quick and easy to cook – just make sure it's cooked all the way through '

JUSTINE REDFEARN, SAINSBURY'S FOOD SAFETY TEAM

Golden lamb hotpot

Try topping this tasty dish with mashed potato to make it into that
old family favourite, shepherd's pie

1 tbsp olive oil

300g Sainsbury's
diced lamb

1 small red onion,
finely chopped

2 garlic cloves, crushed

300g swede, cubed

300g carrots, cut
into small chunks

1 tbsp Sainsbury's
tomato purée

1 tbsp plain flour

1 tbsp fresh thyme leaves

500ml pack Sainsbury's
Signature vegetable stock,
hot, topped up with boiling
water to make 600ml

600g Sainsbury's red
potatoes, skin on,
finely sliced

25g unsalted butter

1 Preheat the oven to 180°C, fan 160°C, gas 4. Heat the oil in
a 2.5-litre ovenproof casserole and sear the lamb in batches
until browned all over (as each batch is done, set it aside on a
plate covered with greasepoof paper).

2 Add the onion and garlic to the casserole and cook gently
for 4-5 mins until softened. Stir in the swede and carrots, and
toss well with the onion and garlic for 1 min. Stir in the tomato
purée, flour and thyme, then return the lamb to the casserole.
Pour over the vegetable stock and bring to the boil, then
remove from the heat.

3 Arrange the potato slices in a circular pattern to completely
cover the top of the meat and vegetable mixture. Dot all over
with small pieces of the butter.

4 Cook, uncovered, for 50-60 mins until the meat and
vegetables are very tender and the potato topping is golden
and crispy on the edges.

5 To freeze, make up to the end of step 2, leave to cool
completely, then cover with cling film and then foil. Freeze for
up to 1 month. Defrost (overnight in the fridge is best), then
continue from step 3.

**For toddlers, cool and cut up to the correct size for your
little one, then serve with a green vegetable, such as
broccoli. For baby, purée to the right consistency.**

 Suitable for freezing

Roasted veg sauce with penne and mozzarella

As this makes enough sauce for two meals, you get great value out of this dish and have another meal ready to go when you need it!

1 red pepper, deseeded
1 courgette
1 onion
500g butternut squash
4 tomatoes, quartered
2 garlic cloves
1 tbsp olive oil
300g Sainsbury's
penne pasta
½ x 160g pack
Sainsbury's Italian cubetti
di pancetta with herbs
75g fresh breadcrumbs
125g ball mozzarella

1 Preheat the oven to 220ºC, fan 200ºC, gas 7. Chop the pepper, courgette, onion and squash into 3cm pieces. Place in a roasting tin with the tomatoes and garlic cloves, then drizzle with the oil. Roast for 40 mins, stirring occasionally, then remove from the oven.

2 Spoon the vegetables into a blender and blitz with 300ml water, until you have a smooth and thick sauce. You only need half the amount of sauce for this recipe, so put the rest in the fridge for 48 hours or freeze for up to 1 month.

3 Cook the pasta in boiling water according to the pack instructions, then drain.

4 Meanwhile, make the topping by frying the pancetta in a non-stick pan for 5 mins. Add the breadcrumbs, then cook for a further 5 mins until the mixture turns golden. Mix the pasta with the sauce, tear in the mozzarella and heat through. Add the breadcrumb topping, then serve.

For toddlers, cut the penne to the right size for your little one.

❄ **Suitable for freezing (see p7 for information)**

Tip...
If you like, you can omit the pancetta and breadcrumb topping to reduce the salt levels for your little ones.

Easy roast pork with prune and sage stuffing

This makes a really easy Sunday roast. Serve it with plenty of veg – steam them to help preserve all their vitamins and nutrients

1 Sainsbury's outdoor
reared British pork
crackling loin joint
(about 870g)
A little salt
500g Sainsbury's
new potatoes

FOR THE STUFFING
1 tbsp olive oil
1 red onion, finely chopped
1 garlic clove,
finely chopped
100g Sainsbury's ready-to
eat prunes, chopped
into small pieces
6 fresh sage leaves, sliced

1 Preheat the oven to 220°C, fan 200°C, gas 7.
Dry the skin of the meat with kitchen paper, then
sprinkle with a little salt and leave for 20 mins.
2 For the stuffing, heat the oil in a frying pan, add
the onion and garlic, and sauté gently for 5 mins
until soft. Add the prunes and sage, season with
black pepper and mix together.
3 Open the meat out and rest skin-side down on
a chopping board. Cut into the thick part of the
meat to open up a pocket and spread over the
stuffing. Roll up and tie with 2 pieces of kitchen
string, then place in a large roasting tin.
4 Roast for 25 mins, then lower the oven
temperature to 200°C, fan 180°C, gas 6. Halve the
potatoes and arrange in the roasting tin and roast
for a further 25 mins per 500g meat or until
cooked all the way through. For a 870g joint, total
cooking time will be about 1 hour 10 mins.
5 Leave for 10 mins to rest, then carve into thin
slices. Serve with stuffing, potatoes and some
steamed veg.
**For toddler and baby portions, remove the fat
and crackling. For baby, purée some pork with
stuffing and vegetables to the right consistency.**

Chocolate fudge brownies

Brownies are delicious served hot with ice cream for pudding, or just as they are, rich and gooey. Freeze slices in freezer bags. Defrost thoroughly and serve at room temperature. These are suitable for toddlers from 18 months

80g butter, plus extra for greasing

Flour, for baking

100g Sainsbury's milk chocolate, broken into pieces

225g light soft brown sugar

1 tsp Sainsbury's Taste the Difference Madagascan vanilla extract

3 medium free-range eggs

180g self-raising flour

1 tbsp cocoa powder

1 Preheat the oven to 180°C, fan 160°C, gas 4. Grease and lightly flour a 22cm x 3-4cm deep square cake tin.
2 Put 80g butter and the chocolate in a bowl that fits snugly over a pan of gently simmering water and stir occasionally until melted. Remove from the heat, then add the sugar, vanilla extract and eggs, and mix well. Sift in the flour and cocoa powder and carefully fold in until just mixed.
3 Pour into the prepared tin. Bake for 20-22 mins – the middle will still be slightly gooey. Leave to cool in the tin, then cut into squares.
For toddlers, serve when cooled.

 Suitable for freezing (see p7 for information)

SERVES 2 ADULTS +
4 TODDLERS
PREP TIME: 10 MINS

Nectarine and raspberry tart

This easy-to-make, no-cook tart is super-fast to prepare and will keep in the fridge for 24 hours. Use low-sugar jam for a healthier version

200ml Sainsbury's natural yogurt

1 tbsp lemon curd or low-sugar raspberry jam

1 Sainsbury's sweet pastry case

3 ripe fresh nectarines or peaches

150g raspberries

2 tbsp low-sugar raspberry jam or ordinary jam

Icing sugar, to decorate

1 Mix the yogurt and lemon curd or jam together in a bowl, then spoon into the pastry case.

2 Cut the nectarines or peaches in half, remove the stones, then slice lengthways and cut each slice in half again widthways. Arrange the nectarine or peach pieces and raspberries on top of the yogurt mixture.

3 Melt the jam with 2 tsp water in a small saucepan, spoon over the fruit and leave to cool before serving. Dust with icing sugar to serve.

For toddlers, cut up to the right size and let them tackle this with their fingers!

" Ella is quite happy as long as she's eating. I'm forever discovering half-eaten snacks around the house "

**Emma Söderholm,
Mum to Ella, 14 months**

Healthier snacking

Snack time
for little ones

My story

'We're really lucky that Ella loves fruit to snack on... unlike her big bro Angelo who likes biscuits – and knows how to ask for them!'

**Emma Söderholm,
Mum to Ella, 14 months,
and Angelo, 3**

Hungry kids are not happy kids, and a mid-morning and mid-afternoon snack can help to sustain energy levels until mealtimes. But getting the balance right is important – too many snacks will impact on your child's appetite for meals, especially if he's a fussy eater. And snacking on too much unhealthy food can lead to excess weight gain.

The key is to make sure snack-time is as nutritious as his main meal. If you wouldn't serve him a plate of crisps or a couple of biscuits for his lunch, then don't give them to him as a mid-morning snack. Think of snacks as a chance to get some vital nutrients inside him. Growing children need lots of calories, especially if they are very active.

It's true that crisps will provide energy, but they won't offer anything in terms of nutrition. If your child snacks on apple chunks and full-fat cheese instead, he'll be upping his calcium intake, which is essential for healthy bones, and getting a boost of vitamins A and C.

Munching on sweets or biscuits will not provide your child with the vitamins and minerals they need. Swap them for oatcakes spread with peanut butter for protein, fibre and healthy monounsaturated fat. Or choose carrot sticks and houmous for protein and a vitamin boost, essential for healthy growth.

The good drinks guide

Water and milk are great drinks for kids. Children also like fruit juice, which can boost vitamin C intake – but be aware that it's also high in sugar and can contribute towards tooth decay and erosion. Dilute it with water (one part juice to 10 parts water) and only give it to your child at mealtimes.

A cup of freshly squeezed orange juice sipped while he's eating his breakfast cereal can help him absorb iron. But don't give squash or cartons of juice as his main drink – give water or milk instead. Increasingly diluting their juice with water can help to wean little ones off it and protect teeth.

Drinking milk helps him towards his three portions of calcium a day – remember, he needs the full-fat variety as a main drink until he's two. Avoid or limit sugary or fizzy drinks.

Savvy snack shopping

Working out which in-between-meal nibbles are best for your child isn't easy. Here are some tips to make sure he's getting his nutrients – and eating something tasty

When it comes to snacking, it pays to read the labels. 'Fruity' or 'fruit-flavoured' doesn't necessarily mean the product contains any fruit at all. Some cereal bars contain more sugar than an equivalent-size chocolate bar and can be more salty, too. Savoury baked snacks may seem healthier than crisps – just check the salt content.

Packaged foods are useful for days out, but you could easily fill up a small airtight container with a selection of your child's favourites to nibble on – veggie sticks, cherry tomatoes, houmous, strawberries and grapes.

Planning ahead and taking healthy snacks with you when you're out and about can also help stave off pester power! And healthy snacks will keep school chidren going between breakfast and lunchtime.

1 A slice of malt loaf with a scraping of butter
It's healthier than cake – top it with fruit to make it even better and to add a little variety.

2 Breadsticks or crackers
A crunchy alternative to crisps – make sure they're reduced salt – and choose wholegrain varieties.

3 Smoothies made with milk, banana slices and strawberry
Fill them up with their favourite fruits, plus milk so they get their calcium and other important nutrients.

4 Frozen bananas
Cut in pieces or mash, then freeze – it tastes just like banana ice cream!

5 Home-made ice-lollies
Make them from fruit smoothies and keep them in the freezer to hand out on hot summer days.

6 Celery boats
Cut sticks of celery and fill with peanut butter or cream cheese.

7 Dried fruit
There are lots of dried fruits to choose from and they're all nutrient packed. A small handful is a good portion size for little ones.

8 Veggie sticks for dipping
Batons of carrot, cucumber, or pepper with low-fat soft cheese or guacamole to dip.

Tip...
Instead of fingers,
you could try
cutting these into
fun shapes
with biscuit
cutters.

Cheese and sesame pastry sticks ⓥ

These freeze well in freezer bags for up to six months. Defrost thoroughly before serving at room temperature

40g butter, chilled and cut into little cubes, plus a little extra for greasing
45g plain flour, plus a little extra for dusting
45g wholemeal flour
30g Sainsbury's British Cheddar, grated
2-3 tbsp Sainsbury's sesame seeds
1 large free-range egg, beaten

1 Preheat the oven to 180°C, fan 160°C, gas 4. Lightly grease a baking sheet or line with greaseproof paper.

2 In a large bowl, rub the butter into the flours until the mixture resembles fine breadcrumbs. Add the grated cheese and 1 tbsp of the sesame seeds, and mix together.

3 Add half the beaten egg and stir into the flour until the mixture starts to come together, then use your hand to work it into a ball.

4 Sprinkle some extra flour onto the work surface and use a rolling pin to roll out half the dough into a rectangle about 4mm thick. Cut widthways into thick finger shapes. Carefully lift them onto the baking sheet, leaving a little space between them. Do the same with the other half of the dough.

5 Brush the remaining egg over the top, then sprinkle with the rest of the sesame seeds. Cook for 10-12 mins or until golden.

6 Eat warm, or leave to cool completely and store in an airtight container for up to one week.

 Suitable for freezing

Smoked mackerel pâté

A delicious spread for toast, this will keep in the fridge for two days. Use wholemeal bread for extra goodness

130g pack Sainsbury's
Taste the Difference
smoked mackerel
Juice of $\frac{1}{2}$ lemon
3 tbsp natural yogurt
$\frac{1}{2}$-1 tsp horseradish sauce
4 slices wholemeal bread,
toasted

1 Peel the skin away from the smoked mackerel and check the fish for any small bones.
2 Put the fish in a bowl with the lemon juice, yogurt and horseradish, to taste. Blend with a hand-held blender or mash with a fork, then spread on the toast and cut into fingers. Serve with halved cherry tomatoes.

Perfect for getting little ones used to the stronger taste of oily fish, this provides omega-3, too

ANNIE DENNY, SAINSBURY'S NUTRITIONIST

Milkshakes

Keep up their milk and fruit intake with these
fun ideas, suitable for toddlers over 12 months

RASPBERRY MILKSHAKE

MAKES 4 TODDLER DRINKS

Whizz 125g Sainsbury's probiotic raspberry yogurt and
150g fresh raspberries with 300ml whole milk in a blender
until smooth, then pour into strong plastic beakers.

BANANA AND VANILLA MILKSHAKE

MAKES 4 TODDLER DRINKS

Whizz 2 ripe bananas with ½ tsp Sainsbury's vanilla
extract and 300ml whole milk in a blender until smooth,
then pour into strong plastic beakers.

PEACHY MILKSHAKE

MAKES 4 TODDLER DRINKS

Whizz 2 ripe peaches, stones removed, 1 ripe banana and
300ml whole milk together in a blender until smooth,
then pour into strong plastic beakers.

Emma says: *'The kids absolutely loved the milkshakes and so
did I! They were lovely and sweet from all the fruit and I'm planning
to make more on the weekend.'*

Easy fruit cake

You can freeze slices of this cake in freezer
bags for up to six months

175g unsalted butter,
softened, plus extra
for greasing
175g golden caster sugar
1 capful Sainsbury's Taste
the Difference Madagascan
vanilla extract
3 free-range eggs
150g Sainsbury's luxury
dried fruit mix, or any dried
fruit of your choice
175g self-raising flour
1 tsp baking powder

1 Preheat the oven to 180°C, fan 160°C, gas 4.
Grease a 20cm round, loose-bottomed cake tin
and line the bottom with greaseproof paper.
2 Beat together the butter, sugar and vanilla until
pale. Add the eggs and fruit, and mix well.
3 Fold in the flour and baking powder, then spoon into
the cake tin. Bake for 30 mins, then check – if it is
browning too much, cover with greaseproof paper.
4 Bake for another 15 mins until golden and risen.
Check the cake is cooked by inserting a skewer into
the middle – if it comes out clean, the cake is done.
Leave to cool in the tin for a few mins before
transferring to a cooling rack.

 Suitable for freezing

MAKES 18 SQUARES
PREP TIME: 10 MINS
COOK TIME: 25 MINS,
PLUS COOLING

Fruity flapjacks

These treats are great for tea, picnics and
lunchboxes and are so easy you can get your
older little ones to help you make them

100g unsalted butter

150g Sainsbury's
porridge oats

50g muesli, with no added
salt or sugar

50g Sainsbury's Fairtrade
light soft brown sugar

100g golden syrup

50g dried apricots, sliced

1 granny smith apple,
peeled and grated

1 Preheat the oven to 200°C, fan 180°C, gas 6.
Melt the butter in a large pan over a medium heat.
Remove the pan from the heat and stir in all the
remaining ingredients.

2 Line an 18cm x 28cm baking tray with greaseproof
paper and press the mixture into it. Bake for 25 mins.

3 Remove and score out 18 squares on the surface with
a knife. Cool in the tray before cutting into pieces. Store
for up to one week in an airtight container.

MAKES 30
PREP TIME: 20 MINS
COOK TIME: ABOUT 15
MINS, PLUS COOLING

Mini carrot & apple muffins

These little muffins are really moist
and delicious, with just a hint of cinnamon

175g plain flour

1 tsp baking powder

½ tsp ground cinnamon

¼ tsp bicarbonate of soda

¼ tsp salt

2 free-range eggs

100g Sainsbury's Fairtrade
light soft brown sugar

65g Sainsbury's
vegetable oil

135g carrots,
coarsely grated

1 medium apple, peeled,
cored and coarsely grated

1 Preheat the oven to 180°C, fan 160°C, gas 4. Arrange
30 paper mini muffin cases on a large baking sheet.

2 Sift the first 5 ingredients into a medium bowl and stir
to combine. Set aside.

3 In a separate, larger bowl, whisk together the eggs
and brown sugar until fluffy, then stir in the vegetable
oil and grated carrots and apple.

4 Add the dry ingredients to the wet ingredients, stirring
until just blended. Pour the muffin mixture into the
prepared cases and bake for about 15 mins or until the
tops of the muffins spring back when you touch them.

5 Remove from the oven and leave to cool slightly on
the baking sheet for 10 mins. Transfer to a wire rack to
cool completely.

'Tom loves spending time in the kitchen. We always say it tastes better because he helped make it!'

Emma Atkins, Mum to Tom, 2

Cooking
with kids

Making cooking fun

MY STORY

'Even at 18 months, Holly was clearly excited about Christmas. Before she went to bed on Christmas Eve, we put out biscuits for Father Christmas and the first thing she did when she got up in the morning was go to see whether they'd been eaten.'

**Kath Stathers,
Mum to Holly, 2**

Enjoying the process of cooking and eating with our family and friends is one of life's great pleasures, and it's never too early to start. Cooking with kids is a great way to get them interested – and a great standby rainy day activity for many mums.

Children love to use their hands when cooking, so always start with a good wash with soap and water. However hard you try, it will always be a messy affair, so an apron is a good idea, and sit her at the table so the bowls and ingredients are at the right height. You could also look out for a set of kid-sized utensils that are just for her. Obviously some supervised activities (stirring on a hob and chopping) are best left for older children (from around seven and up, depending on the child), but you can get toddlers involved (with your help) in weighing out ingredients and mixing raw ingredients in a bowl.

Start simple

Flapjacks are easy to start with (there's a recipe you can try on p158), and you could experiment with adding extras such as seeds, dried fruit or chocolate chips.

Children also love to make muffins, bread rolls and cup cakes especially if they get to decorate them too.

Try home-made mini pizzas, too – as well as helping to mix the pizza dough, they can choose their own toppings (see our recipe on p34). Younger children aren't great at waiting, so speed up the process by using halved muffins as bases – toast in the oven before letting them decorate with tomato purée, tuna chunks, sweetcorn and grated cheese (or whatever she prefers) then toast under the grill. Milkshakes are also

However hard you try, it will always be a messy affair...

A LEARNING EXPERIENCE

Cooking helps children find out all about ingredients and what food is made of, but it teaches them a whole lot more, too.

Weighing, measuring and timing is a great introduction to basic maths. Pouring and mixing help with hand-eye co-ordination. They'll also learn how to follow instructions, a skill they'll find essential once they start school. Why not start a 'family favourite recipe book' and get older children writing, and younger children drawing pictures to decorate the pages.

MY STORY

'Tom is naturally curious about cooking so I try to get him involved as much as possible. We love baking together and he's become a pro at mixing and pouring. He even helped make a birthday cake for his big sister Laurie. The kitchen does get a bit messy but that's just part of the fun. He's my mini master chef!'

**Emma Atkins,
Mum to Tom, 2**

eat for (nearly) instant atification (try our ideas p154). Even children who e too young to chop the it can select their own mbinations for Mum or d to whizz up.

afety first

etting your kids involved in e kitchen is a great way to t them interested in food. aching them good kitchen bits from the start is valuable, so outline the fety and hygiene rules d why some items in the chen could be dangerous m the outset. The key message is that cooking should be fun but safe!

Get your child familiar with hand washing before, during and after cooking, including after touching pets or raw foods and going to the toilet. One of the ways they will learn safety and hygiene is by watching you, so make sure you are demonstrating good kitchen habits, too. See p6-7 for more on hygiene and food safety.

Supervision at all times is essential. Younger children obviously need to be kept away from ovens, hobs and dangerous utensils without feeling they are missing out, so keep them busy with the mixing spoon! The time-honoured tradition of letting children lick the mixing bowl after making a cake batter is best avoided if raw eggs have been used.

Give them the freedom to decide what to make and let them use their imagination, whether this is inventing their own sandwich filling or deciding how to decorate the tops of cakes. Getting kids involved with food from an early age is a great part of their development, but always make sure it's safe.

Little green fingers

Learning about where food comes from helps kids understand the importance of good nutrition, and gets them excited about cooking – and eating. Get them growing, in more ways than one!

Grow your own

Eating your greens is definitely more appealing if you've helped to grow them! Kids love getting involved in the garden, and it helps them learn where food comes from, and find out the different ways that fruit and vegetables grow. Letting them help with weeding, digging, planting, watering and, of course, harvesting, is great for hand-eye co-ordination (remember to always make sure that everyone's hands are washed after you've finished gardening, even if gloves have been worn). And gardening is like a nature lesson - they'll be fascinated when they find worms and woodlice in the soil, and can witness for themselves the importance of water and sunlight.

You don't need an allotment to grow your own - your kids will love watching the progress of the strawberries, carrots, peas, beans and other produce they helped to plant in a sunny patch in the garden. If you've got the space, you could give pre-schoolers their own little patch and let them choose what to grow in it.

Grow-bags are great for courtyards and even balconies - plant lettuce, tomatoes and cucumber for fresh salad all summer long - or grow potatoes in a bucket. Or, if you want to start really small, pots on a sunny windowsill are ideal for growing fresh herbs

You won't have to do too much to get children interested, but giving them their own mini set of tools and watering goes down well, as does planting something fast-growing, such as sunflowers or nasturtiums, to keep them interested while they're waiting for the veg to grow.

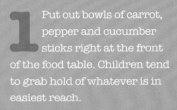

Pots on a windowsill are ideal for growing fresh herbs

1 Put out bowls of carrot, pepper and cucumber sticks right at the front of the food table. Children tend to grab hold of whatever is in easiest reach.

2 Don't bring out the cakes and cookies until the children have had a plate of savoury food.

3 Don't get hung up on finding something for the ultra-fussy child to eat. The party only lasts a few hours, so they won't go hungry for very long!

4 Make healthier 'pizzas' by using halved wholemeal muffins as a base – top them with tomato purée and mozzarella, then grill.

5 Sausages are always a big hit – wrap in puff pastry before baking for home-made sausage rolls.

Party time!

It wouldn't be a party without yummy cakes or dessert, but you can also add some healthy but delicious savouries for balance. Here are our tried-and-tested tips for the perfect party feast

6 Fill wholemeal wraps with houmous and grated cheese, egg mayonnaise or tuna and sweetcorn with mayonnaise, then roll up and cut chunks at an angle for an appealing alternative to sandwiches.

7 Make your own home-made chicken nuggets by frying chopped pieces of cooked chicken breasts in breadcrumbs.

8 'Make your own pizza' parties go down well with older kids – give each child a prepared base to decorate and let them choose from a selection of ingredients.

9 Set some tinned peaches or pears in jelly and serve with ice cream for a refreshing party dessert.

10 Potato wedges, roasted in olive oil, are great for older kids (not to mention adults!). Serve with a yogurt and cucumber, or mildly spicy tomato salsa dip.

11 Ice-cream factories are also great fun for kids – give each child a bowl of vanilla ice cream, then let them add their own toppings from bowls of chopped up strawberries, mini marshmallows, Smarties or M&Ms, chocolate sprinkles or hundreds and thousands, and squirty chocolate or strawberry sauce.

12 Have a few jugs of well-diluted fruit squash handy – all that running around makes kids really thirsty! Add some slices of orange and apple.

MY STORY
'For Jessica's first birthday we invited the whole family over for a little party. I try not to give Jessica too many sweet things but, as it was a special day, I made a big cake in the shape of a one and spent ages icing it. It was a real hit and Jessica's dad was on hand to video the candles being blown out.'

Abigail Diggines, Mum to Jessica, 12 months

Top tables

Part of the excitement and fun of a celebration is the special attention paid to the table – kids love all the little extras that come out at party time. Look out for special plates, colourful cups and other fun tableware at Sainsbury's. Bright paper tablecloths or placemats and serviettes with fun designs are perfect for kids' parties and create a sense of occasion, which helps to get kids interested in the food on offer.

Domino biscuits

Toddlers and pre-schoolers will love making these – not only
are they delicious but you can also play dominoes with them!

100g unsalted butter,
chilled and cut into cubes
150g plain flour
1 tbsp cocoa powder
60g golden caster sugar
2 tbsp milk (or 1 free-range
egg yolk)
75g pack Silver Spoon
Coloured Choco Beans
or chocolate chips,
to decorate

1 Preheat the oven to 180°C, fan 160°C, gas 4.
In a mixing bowl, rub the butter into the flour until
it resembles breadcrumbs. Add the cocoa powder
and sugar, and mix together. Add the milk (or egg
yolk) and mix together. Add a little more flour if
the dough is still sticky, and roll into a ball.
2 Roll the dough out to 3mm thickness, then trim the
edges to make a neat rectangle and cut into long
strips that are 3cm wide. Cut the strips into 6cm
lengths and score a line (without cutting
all the way through) across the middle of each
3cm x 6cm rectangle. Re-roll the trimmings and cut to
make more dominoes.
3 Place on a baking sheet and decorate with the
chocolate beans or chips to make the domino
numbers – for example, put 2 dots on one half and 3
on the other. Bake for 8-10 mins. Allow to cool, then
play dominoes as you eat!

 Suitable for freezing (see p7 for information)

" *With this recipe, your little ones will learn
all the basic skills used in baking* "

ANNIE DENNY, SAINSBURY'S NUTRITIONIST

Birthday tea

Birthday parties are a big event for little ones – and their parents!
Here are some ideas to make the celebration deliciously special...

Starry pizza bites ⓥ

MAKES 16
PREP TIME: 15 MINS
COOK TIME: 10-15 MINS

Preheat the oven to 180°C, fan 160°C, gas 4. Use an 8cm star-shaped pastry cutter to cut out 2 stars each from 8 slices of white or wholemeal bread. Brush each side of the bread with a little oil and bake on a baking sheet in the top of the oven for 5 mins or until just golden. Turn the stars over and top each one with a little Sainsbury's SO organic pomodoro pasta sauce and a small piece of Sainsbury's mozzarella. Bake for a further 4-6 mins until the cheese is melted and serve warm.

Jellies with clementines

SERVES 8
PREP TIME: 5-10 MINS, PLUS CHILLING

Make up a 135g pack of orange jelly in a jug according to the pack instructions. Peel 3 clementines, separate the segments and remove any white pith. Take 8 small plastic dessert dishes and put 2 clementine segments into the bottom of each one. Pour over enough jelly to cover the segments, but not so much that they float. Put the dishes in the fridge until the jelly is set, but keep the jug of jelly at room temperature. Repeat two more times, layering the clementines and putting the dishes in the fridge to set until all the jelly is used up. This will take a while, so it's best to make them the day before serving, if you can.

Popcorn garlands

MAKES 8 GARLANDS
PREP TIME: 30 MINS
COOK TIME: 5 MINS

Sift 2 tbsp icing sugar into a large bowl. Heat 2 tsp vegetable oil in a pan over a high heat until very hot, add 100g popping corn and cover. Shake the pan around for 30 secs, then switch off the heat. The heat of the pan will finish popping all the corn. When it has subsided, remove the lid. Add the popcorn to the bowl and mix well. To colour the popcorn, push 50g raspberries through a sieve, and collect the juice. Put a teaspoonful into a bowl and add half of the popcorn and stir to colour all over. Cut a length of elastic and thread the coloured and plain popcorn on alternately (we suggest adults use a large, sterilised sewing needle to do this). Add halved dried ready-to-eat apricots in between the popcorn, if you like.

Mini berry tarts

MAKES 24 TARTS
PREP TIME: 20 MINS,
PLUS CHILLING
COOK TIME: 13-15 MINS

Put 225g plain flour into a bowl. Cut 115g chilled unsalted butter into small pieces and rub into the flour. Stir in 1 tsp golden caster sugar. Mix in 1 egg yolk and 1-2 tbsp water a little at a time, until the pastry comes together. Form into a ball, wrap in clingfilm and chill for 30 mins. Preheat the oven to 200ºC, fan 180ºC, gas 6. Sprinkle your work surface and rolling pin with flour and roll the pastry out to about 3mm thick. Cut out 24 circles with a 10cm fluted pastry cutter and put them in 2 x 12-hole mini tart trays. Prick the base of each once with a fork. Bake for 10-15 mins until golden. Remove from the oven, allow to cool slightly then fill with fresh berries of your choice. To finish, warm 1 tsp reduced-sugar strawberry or blackcurrant jam in a pan over a low heat and brush over the berries. Dust the tarts with icing sugar before serving.

Chocolate and vanilla marble cake

This all-in-one marble cake is simple to make and looks great for a birthday celebration

225g unsalted butter, softened, plus extra for greasing
225g golden caster sugar
1 capful Sainsbury's Taste the Difference Madagascan vanilla extract
4 free-range eggs
200g self-raising flour
1 tsp baking powder
1 tbsp milk (if required)
30g cocoa powder

FOR THE ICING
200g icing sugar
2 tbsp cocoa powder
Jelly drops, fudge chunks, sprinkles and happy birthday candles, to decorate

1 Preheat the oven to 180°C, fan 160°C, gas 4. Grease a 20cm square cake tin with butter and line the base with greaseproof paper.
2 Put the butter, caster sugar, vanilla extract and eggs into a large bowl. Sift the flour and baking powder into the bowl and beat together with an electric hand whisk until combined. Don't overbeat or the cake won't rise. If the mixture seems too stiff, add 1 tbsp milk to loosen.
3 Dot half of the mixture randomly in the cake tin, leaving some gaps. Sift the cocoa into the remaining cake mixture in the bowl, mix together, then spoon into the gaps in the tin. Drag the handle of a spoon gently through the mixture once or twice to create a marble effect.
4 Bake for 40-45 mins or until cooked and a skewer inserted into the centre comes out clean. Remove from the tin, turn out onto a wire rack, remove the greaseproof paper and allow to cool, then transfer to a serving plate.
5 Mix together the icing sugar, cocoa and 3 tbsp water until you have a smooth icing, then spread over the cake. Decorate the top with the sweets and birthday candles.

Pesto Christmas tree shapes Ⓥ

These are so easy to make with your little ones and are a tasty savoury treat for the festive season

Butter, for greasing
(optional)
½ x 500g pack Sainsbury's
shortcrust pastry
4 tsp Sainsbury's classic
Italian pesto
Flour, for dusting

1 Preheat the oven to 180ºC, fan 160ºC, gas 4.
2 Line 2 baking trays with greaseproof paper or grease with a little butter.
3 Soften the pastry a little with your hands, then add 2 tsp of the pesto and squash it into the pastry. Knead the pastry lightly to mix in the pesto. Sprinkle a little flour onto the work surface and, using a rolling pin, roll out half the pastry until about 3mm thick.
4 Cut out Christmas tree shapes with a pastry cutter and put onto the trays. Repeat with the remaining pastry.
5 Brush the remaining pesto over the trees and bake for 10 mins or until just golden brown and cooked.

MAKES ABOUT 35
SMALL BISCUITS
PREP TIME: 15 MINS,
PLUS CHILLING
COOK TIME: 10 MINS

Gingerbread men

A fun treat to put out for Santa and his reindeer!
You'll need a 7cm gingerbread cutter for this recipe

50g butter, plus extra, for
greasing (optional)
240g plain flour, plus extra
for dusting
1½ tsp bicarbonate of soda
1 tsp ground ginger
Pinch of cinnamon
1 free-range egg
85g Sainsbury's Fairtrade
light soft brown sugar

2 tbsp Sainsbury's
golden syrup
1 tbsp treacle
Finely grated zest of
½ orange
About 100g icing sugar,
to decorate
About 20g currants for the
buttons, to decorate

1 Preheat the oven to 180°C, fan 160°C, gas 4. Line 3
baking sheets with greaseproof paper or grease the
trays with a little butter.
2 Put the flour, bicarbonate of soda, ginger and
cinnamon into a mixing bowl.
3 Cut the 50g butter into small pieces and rub it into
the dry ingredients with your fingertips until the
mixture resembles breadcrumbs.
4 Crack the egg into a jug, add the sugar, syrup,
treacle and orange zest, and mix together. Add this
to the flour and stir to combine. Use your hands to
squeeze the mixture together and shape into a ball.
5 Knead the dough on a lightly floured work surface
for 1-2 mins until smooth. Wrap in clingfilm and rest in
the fridge for 10 mins.

6 Sprinkle a little more flour over the work surface
and roll out about a quarter of the dough to about
5mm thick, then cut out small gingerbread men and
put the biscuits onto the baking sheets. Repeat with
the remaining dough. Bake for 10 mins until golden.
Let them cool for a few mins, then put them onto a
wire rack to cool completely.
7 Mix the icing sugar with about 1 tbsp water and use,
with the currants, to decorate your gingerbread men.

 Suitable for freezing (see p7 for information)

Easy peasy coconut ice

Kids will love getting their hands messy with this ice mix! Put the ices into Cellophane bags and tie with a ribbon for a lovely edible gift

Butter, for greasing
397g tin condensed milk
300g Sainsbury's desiccated coconut
300g icing sugar
1 capful Sainsbury's Taste the Difference Madagascan vanilla extract
Few drops of red (or pink) food colouring

1 Grease and line a 24cm square cake tin.

2 Pour the condensed milk into a bowl, then add the coconut, icing sugar and vanilla. Mix until well combined. Spoon half of the mixture into the tin and press down firmly.

3 Add a few drops of the food colouring to the remaining mixture. Mix until you have an even colour.

4 Spoon the red mixture over the top of the white layer and smooth with a palette knife or spatula.

5 Cover, put in a cool place and leave to set for at least 4 hours or overnight.

6 Cut into squares and wrap up 4-5 pieces at a time in Cellophane gift bags, sealed with ribbon and personalised gift tags.

Easter cookies

Like a hot cross bun in biscuit form, these fragrant,
spicy cookies are perfect for an Easter tea-time treat

125g unsalted butter,
softened, plus extra
for greasing (optional)
Finely grated zest of ½
orange, plus 2 tbsp juice
1 tsp mixed spice
200g Sainsbury's Fairtrade
light soft brown sugar
1 capful Sainsbury's Taste
the Difference Madagascan
vanilla extract
200g self-raising flour
200g mixed dried fruit

1 Preheat the oven to 180°C, fan 160°C, gas 4.
Grease 3 baking trays or line with greaseproof paper.
If you don't have 3 trays, bake them in batches.
2 In a bowl, beat the butter, orange zest, mixed spice
and sugar together until pale and fluffy.
3 Add the vanilla extract, sift in the flour, then add the
dried fruit and orange juice, and mix well.
4 Form the mixture into small balls using a teaspoon
and put onto the baking trays, spacing well apart.
They will spread and flatten into cookies as they bake.
5 Bake for 10-13 mins until cooked and light golden,
but still chewy inside. Leave to cool.

 Suitable for freezing (see p7 for information)

Chocolate crispy mountains

Chocolate crispy mountains

MAKES 6. PREP TIME: 10 MINS

Melt 100g Sainsbury's milk chocolate in a bowl (parents can do this in a microwave
or over a separate bowl of hot water). Mix in 50g rice pops until they are covered
in chocolate. Spoon the mixture into 6 brightly coloured baking cases placed inside
muffin tins to help them keep their shape. Put a few Smarties over each chocolate
mountain, then let them set in the fridge for 30 mins before eating.

Halloween eyeballs Ⓥ

Scary treats never tasted so good! These savoury dough balls will be gobbled up in no time

145g pack Sainsbury's pizza base mix

Flour, for dusting

4 tsp sundried tomato paste, tomato purée or Sainsbury's

Italian red pepper purée

12 Sainsbury's Basics mozzarella pearls

6 pitted black olives, halved

1 Make up the pizza dough mixture according to the pack instructions. Add a little extra flour if the mix is quite sticky, and bring together with your hands until it forms a ball.

2 Knead well on a floured surface for 5 mins until smooth and elastic, then break into 12 pieces. Roll each piece into a ball and put on a non-stick baking tray.

3 Make a deep hole in the middle of each ball with your finger, then dot some tomato paste or purée into the hole. Press a mozzarella ball into the hole, then push half an olive on top of that. Repeat with the other balls. Leave in a warm place to rise for 20 mins. Meanwhile, preheat the oven to 200ºC, fan 180ºC, gas 6.

4 Push the olives gently to squash them back into the dough balls and bake for 15 mins until cooked. If some of the olives have fallen off, poke these back in after cooking. They will look quite scary!

SERVES 6 TODDLERS
PREP TIME: 5 MINS
COOK TIME: 5 MINS

Witches' juice

Your little ones will love this bewitching brew, guaranteed to warm them up for Halloween!

300ml cranberry juice
300ml fresh orange juice
6 cinnamon sticks

1 Put the juices and cinnamon sticks into a saucepan and heat gently until it is just warm, not hot. Pour into heat-proof plastic tumblers and put a cinnamon stick in each cup. Tell toddlers it's 'witches' juice' – they'll love it!

Try...
Use extra-thick double cream instead of yogurt for an indulgent treat!

Swiss roll with fresh raspberries

This is one Dad and little ones can make together for Mum's special day. If you prefer, you could use strawberries instead

Butter, for greasing
3 free-range eggs
85g golden caster sugar, plus extra to decorate
1 capful Sainsbury's Taste the Difference Madagascan vanilla extract
Zest of 1/2 lemon
85g self-raising flour
3 tbsp raspberry or strawberry jam
3 or 4 tbsp Sainsbury's natural Greek-style yogurt or half-fat crème fraîche
100g fresh raspberries, to decorate

1 Preheat the oven to 180°C, fan 160°C, gas 4.

2 Grease and line a 30cm x 24cm Swiss roll tin with greaseproof paper.

3 Use an electric hand whisk to beat the eggs, sugar, vanilla and lemon zest in a bowl until pale, fluffy and thick. This will take at least 3-5 mins.

4 Sift the flour onto the creamed mixture and carefully fold in using a large metal spoon. Pour into the tin, smooth the surface with a spatula and bake for 12 mins.

5 While it's still hot, invert the cake onto a sheet of greaseproof paper sprinkled with extra caster sugar on a work top. Peel away the paper you used to line the tin and put a fresh sheet of greaseproof paper on top of the cake.

6 Using the bottom piece of paper to help you, roll the cake up widthways to make a swiss roll.

7 When it is cool, unroll, remove the paper and spread the cake with the jam, then top with the yogurt or crème fraîche and raspberries and roll up. Sprinkle with golden caster sugar and extra raspberries to decorate.

Lemon and strawberry cream biscuits

These little treats have lots of fresh strawberry and lemon flavours. Fun for kids to help make, they look wonderful on an afternoon tea table

100g unsalted
butter, softened
50g golden caster sugar
1 capful Sainsbury's Taste
the Difference Sicilian
lemon extract
140g self-raising flour

FOR THE
STRAWBERRY CREAM
2 medium, ripe
strawberries
50g unsalted
butter, softened
150g icing sugar
Few drops Sainsbury's
Taste the Difference
Sicilian lemon extract
(optional)

1 Preheat the oven to 180ºC, fan 160ºC, gas 4. Lightly grease 2 large baking trays (or line them with greaseproof paper).

2 Put the butter and sugar into a bowl. Add the lemon extract and beat together with a wooden spoon until pale.

3 Tip the flour into the bowl then mix it all together – it's easy and fun if your toddler uses their hands for this stage.

4 Mould the mixture into 28 small walnut-size balls. The younger your child, the less likely it is that you will have perfectly round biscuits - be prepared for any shape!

5 Arrange on the baking trays - leaving enough space between to allow them to spread - and bake for 12 mins until golden. Keep an eye on them as you don't want them to go brown. Cool on the tray then transfer to a wire rack.

6 To make the strawberry cream filling, wash and hull the strawberries and put into a bowl. Give your toddler a masher to squash the berries to a pulp - they'll love this bit!

7 Add the soft butter, icing sugar and lemon extract (if using) to the strawberries, and beat together with a wooden spoon. You may need to add more icing sugar (this will vary depending on how juicy your strawberries are).

8 Spoon a little cream on the base of a biscuit and sandwich with another biscuit and serve.

No-bake fudge marshmallows

Little chefs will love helping to make these for Dad.
They're quite rich, so a little bit goes a long way

2 x 200g Sainsbury's
Belgian cooking
milk chocolate
397g tin Nestlé
Carnation Caramel
150g Sainsbury's
marshmallows
100g mini marshmallows

1 Line a 20cm x 20cm square baking tin with greaseproof paper.
2 Break the chocolate into pieces and place in a microwave-safe bowl. Add the Carnation Caramel and stir.
3 Microwave on medium-high for 1 min, remove from the microwave and stir. Return the bowl to the microwave and continue to cook until the chocolate has melted. Parents should do this bit.
4 Stir until the mixture is smooth, then add the marshmallows, mixing well. Quickly spread the mixture into the lined tin and finish by sprinkling the top with mini marshmallows. Do your best to really stick them into the fudge so they set while it is in the fridge. Chill for at least 3 hours, then lift out of the tin and cut into cubes to serve.

Emma says: *'Tom loved making this for his Dad – I had to keep an eye on him though, as I think more marsmallows went in his mouth than in the bowl! The hardest part was waiting for it to set!'*

Thanks for sharing

The Little ones parent panel allows new mums and dads to share their experiences. These are just some of the families who've taken part – telling their stories, swapping tips, testing products and recipes, and seeking answers to common parenting problems...

Maria Onyango and Theo

James and Kim Nelson, and twins Harry and Cora

Keely and Edward Hart, and Dan...

Caroline and Mike Luck, and Ollie

Amy King and Bella

Lorraine Armstrong-Gould and Sander

Special thanks to these and all the other parents who helped put this book together, including Julie Schippers, Melanie Holmes, Linda Sutherland, Yvette Newbatt, Catherine Edwards, Jade Walkley, Sunita Parmar, Abigail Diggines, Owen Blagrove and Kath Stathers.

Sarah and Sanjay Singh,
Rohan and Layla

Jenny and Craig Breadmore,
Daisy and Ruby

Helen Kettle
and Seb

Emma Söderholm,
Angelo and Ella

...join the Little ones baby & toddler
club at www.sainsburys.co.uk/littleones

Lucy Howe
and Freddie

Sarah Wilson
and Charlotte

Emma Atkins
and Tom

Katie Millan
and Carrie

Index

Credits

Editor Julie Stevens
Consultant editors (Sainsbury's)
Annie Denny and Justine Redfearn
**Consultant editor (British
Nutrition Foundation)**
Sara Stanner
Sub-editor Ward Hellewell
Assistant editor
Lauren Hoffman
Writer Sally Brown
Nutritional analysis
Fiona Hunter
Indexing Patricia Baker

Food

Senior food editor
Georgina Fuggle
Food assistant
Mima Sinclair
Food assistant
Hannah Yeadon
Food support
Archie Bashford

Design

Art director
Pam Price
Senior Designer Alex Tait
Designer Tim Mapleston

Account management

Senior account director
Lynne de Lacy
Account executive Amy Fixter
Publishing director
Dorcas Jamieson
Head of content
Helen Renshaw

Pictures

Photographers Terry Benson,
Amanda Heywood and Ian Boddy

Food stylists Mari Williams,
Eliza Baird and Sal Henley
Prop stylist Rob Merrett
Hair & make up Claire Ray

For Sainsbury's

Book team Phil Carroll,
Sharon Nightingale and
Louise Chipps
Director of Sainsbury's Brand
Judith Batchelar
Little Ones team
Rachel Leonard
Health and Safety
Sharon Chambers
Food Safety Nikki Mosley
Baby Team Keely Hart
Own-brand team
Anna Shirley, Lucy Howe and
Tamsin Boardman
Marketing team & PR
Rebecca Singleton, Katarina
Williams and Cath Wilkins
Supply chain
Natalie Sumner and Lee Scott

For British Nutrition Foundation

Emma Williams

Print & production

Production manager
Mike Lamb
Production executive
Katie Harrison
Colour origination F1 Colour
Printers Butler Tanner & Dennis
Ltd, Frome and London

Special thanks to...

Coralyn Barber, Dan Jones,
Richard Jung and
Gareth Morgans

© Produced by Seven Publishing on behalf of Sainsbury's
Supermarkets Ltd, 33 Holborn, London EC1N 3HT.
Published September 2011. All rights reserved. No part of this
publication may be reproduced, stored in a retrieval system or
transmitted in any form by any means electronic, mechanical,
photocopying, recording or otherwise, without the prior written
permission of Seven Publishing. ISBN-13: 978-0956630353

Seven.

MIX
Paper from
responsible sources
FSC® C023561